What Politics is About

What Politics is About

H S Ferns MA, PhD (*Cantab.*)
*Emeritus Professor of Political Science
in the University of Birmingham*

and

K W Watkins BSc (Econ.), PhD (*London*)
*Sometime Reader in Political Theory and Institutions
in the University of Sheffield*

THE SHERWOOD PRESS

First published 1985

©H S Ferns and K W Watkins 1985

The Sherwood Press Ltd, 88 Tylney Road, London E7 0LY

ISBN 0 907671 11 X

Set in Times by Book Ens, Saffron Walden, Essex
Printed and bound by Redwood Burn Ltd., Trowbridge, Wiltshire

Contents

Illustrations

To Maureen and Edith

'Man is by nature a political animal'—
Aristotle (384–322 BC)

Preface

At the heart of politics lies the problem of how men and women achieve their desires and expectations under conditions of relative scarcity when the limited resources of the moment have alternative uses. This fundamental fact has applied throughout history, irrespective of the form of government or the level of economic and technological development at any time or in any place.

Within this basic framework of human relations, men and women seek to obtain and retain power in order to take what they believe to be, rightly or wrongly, the best decisions and to implement them. Those who exercise political power may do so because their authority is accepted by their fellows or because they may resort, or be compelled to resort, to the use of force. In either case it is essential for them to justify themselves and their actions and thus gain legitimacy in their society.

It can be argued that life daily demonstrates that the issues in the real world are always politico-economic in character and that the judgement and actions of people are shaped by their historical and ideological approach to contemporary reality.

Thus politics is about much more than government and administration, parties and elections. It embraces education, information, sciences, technology—in short, the totality of the human situation. Further, it is global in character.

This book endeavours to examine what politics is about in the light of Judeo–Christian, Liberal–Democratic and Marxist attitudes and beliefs. We have drawn upon the experience not only of Britain and Western Europe but also of the United States and the Far East.

A debt is owed to the generations of students upon whom some of the ideas have been inflicted and to friends in the 'real world of politics' for whom practically inclined academics have sometimes proved to be uncomfortable bedfellows.

One of the temptations of political study is dogmatism: that one lot—

my lot—are right and everyone else is wrong. The authors have tried not to forget the words of that great man who flourished in an age of political fanaticism, the Lord Protector Oliver Cromwell: 'I beseech you, in the bowels of Christ, think it possible you may be mistaken.'

H.S.F.
K.W.W.
September 1984

1 Politics is about People

In 1719 Daniel Defoe published *The Life and Strange Adventures of Robinson Crusoe*. This story, not perhaps as well known nowadays as it used to be, is an imagined account of an Englishman cast away on a desert island. For fifteen years Robinson Crusoe laboured alone, building a life for himself. His only companion was a parrot which learned to speak his name. In these lonely circumstances there were no politics because, on Crusoe's island, there was only one human being utterly by himself and, therefore, with no relations with others.

One day, when walking on the shore, Crusoe discovered a human footprint. 'I stood like one thunderstruck, or as if I had seen an apparition,' he wrote. From that moment, and for the next thirteen years, until he escaped from the island, Crusoe faced political problems. Who was this other human being whose footprint he had discovered? Possible friend, or likely enemy?

Until this moment Crusoe's principal problem had been survival: to feed himself and to protect himself from the forces of nature. Now there was another human being or many human beings somewhere, if not on his island, not far away.

He began at once to devise additional protection for himself. He undertook what we would today call an armament programme: to fortify his place of residence, to prepare places to hide and to position his loaded muskets so that he might repel attack. That other human being, whose footprints he had discovered, might be harmless, but equally he might not be. Prudence dictated a defence policy.

Then Crusoe discovered evidence that not just one man but many came ashore on 'his' island, and that they were cannibals. It was now a question of themselves or myself. Crusoe was not sure that his defence policy would work and that he could escape being found and devoured, but he was determined to survive. Therefore he worked to improve his means of doing so.

Crusoe was one man. The cannibals were many. Crusoe's policy for survival was to keep out of their way; to observe them but not to reveal

The frontispiece to the first edition of *Robinson Crusoe* (1719)

his presence and so invite attack. Observation, however, disclosed to him a circumstance which prompted him to change his policy. One of the victims of the cannibals escaped before he could be killed. 'It came now very warmly upon my thoughts,' Crusoe tells us, 'and indeed irresistibly, that now the time had come to get me a servant, and perhaps a companion and assistant—that I was plainly called by Providence to save this poor creature's life.' Accordingly, Crusoe armed himself, and placed himself, between the pursuers and their quarry. One of the cannibals he knocked unconscious, and when another started to string an arrow to his bow, Crusoe shot him dead.

As a result of this encounter Robinson Crusoe created a community of two people: himself and the man to whom he gave the name 'Friday'. He taught 'Friday' to call him Master. At first he did not completely trust Friday, and he always slept behind a closed door, and he kept weapons out of Friday's hands except when he had Friday under his eye. Slowly, however, trust between Crusoe and Friday increased and, although the relationship of master and servant persisted, they learned to live together as friends and companions.

From a population of two, the community on Crusoe's island expanded to four, as a result of releasing two captives from the grip of the cannibals, 'My island was now peopled, and I thought myself very rich in subjects,' Crusoe records, 'And it was a merry reflection which I frequently made, how like a king I looked. First of all the whole country was my own mere property; so that I had an undoubted right to dominion. Secondly, my people were perfectly subjected; I was absolute lord and lawgiver; they all owed their lives to me, and were ready to lay down their lives, if there had been an occasion for it, for me.'

The next stage in the politics of the island resulted in Crusoe's escape and return to England. Another body of men landed on the island; this time English sailors. Like the cannibals, the Englishmen were divided; not between those who ate and those to be eaten, but between the two officers and two passengers who were forcibly in the hands of the crew who had mutinied. Crusoe decided to assist the weaker party, i.e. the officers and the passengers. While the sailors were exploring 'his island', Crusoe approached the officers and made them a proposition. He would deliver them from their enemies on two conditions: '1. That while you stay on this island you will not pretend to any authority here. 2. That if the ship is, or may be, recovered you will carry me and my men to England passage free.'

The four men agreed to these conditions. Crusoe armed them, and together they defeated the mutineers, hanged their leader, and offered the disarmed mutineers the choice of remaining marooned on the island or returning in irons to England to be hanged. The mutineers chose life, and Crusoe and his allies returned to England.

The experience of Robinson Crusoe on his island, as imagined by Daniel Defoe, tells us something about politics. Politics is concerned with the discovery and establishment of the terms and conditions on which people live and work together. Crusoe, Friday, the Portuguese sailor and Friday's father, who were liberated from the cannibals, and the English ship captain, his mate and his passengers all had a common interest which bound them together and made Crusoe into what he liked to think was a king and lawgiver. This common interest was survival in the presence of enemies.

If Crusoe's story tells us something, however, it does not tell us everything about politics. Had Crusoe, the king and lawgiver as he supposed himself to be, decided not to return to England, to remain on his island, to rule over his subjects, and to repel any who invaded his domain, the community created by work and successful political manoeuvring would not have survived. It lacked one essential ingredient of all communities: two sexes. Only if man and woman live together and produce children can there be life. Alone and separate men and women have only one life. In children they live again, and so life continues from the remote past towards what we hope may be a far-off future.

We can see from Crusoe's experience on his desert island that he survived, flourished and eventually escaped because he had bodily strength, intelligence, some tools and supplies saved from the wreck of his ship, and good luck. He had something in addition: courage and the will to live.

Crusoe was a free man because he was alone and there was no-one to check him in anything he did. On the other hand, he was not free to do anything he pleased. He had needs on which he was obliged to expend energy and use his intelligence to satisfy: the need for food, for shelter and for security and protection from animals and eventually from cannibals and mutineers who were members of his own species. Crusoe found freedom, ease and security by working and, when they presented themselves, by solving the political problems of his relations with others who intruded into his island home.

Because there were no women on his island and none was among the visitors to his island, he was not confronted with the consequences of the reproduction of the species, and with the care and nurture of children. For most of his time on his island he had no problems of co-operating with others in the performance of work, and at no time was he confronted with the problem of access to the natural resources of his island. He took what he needed because there were no others present.

In seeking to answer the question, 'What is politics?', why start with a brief account of an imaginary man on an imaginary island? For the same reason that the Bible, which is an account of the origins and development of the Judeo–Christian religion, begins with the story of Adam and Eve in the Garden of Eden. We require a very simple account of social and economic circumstances which enables us to see the essentials of the human activity to which we give the name 'politics'. We are obliged to fix in our minds the character of the problems which political activity seeks to solve.

Thinking about the Robinson Crusoe story, about what Daniel Defoe tells us his hero did and about what he did not tell us, we can come to some preliminary conclusions about the human condition, i.e. the circumstances in which all communities at all times in all places find themselves if they are to survive longer than the lives of the individuals who, at any one time, make up the community. These circumstances we call the natural necessities of men and women.

They are four in number. First, there is the need for food and shelter. Second, there is the need to reproduce the species and to care for and nurture children. Third, there is the need to work in order to satisfy the first two needs on the list. Fourth, there is the need to co-operate together so that men and women can work and assure themselves of access to the natural resources they need.

We cannot be sure how long is the history of the species *homo sapiens*. We do know, however, that for most of human history, in fact until well into the nineteenth century, a very large proportion of the human race were engaged in the task of providing themselves with food and shelter, sufficient in quantity and quality to survive from generation to generation. The existence of cities implies that in communities where they grew up, there was a surplus of food sufficient to feed those who lived in them and were not engaged in agricultural or pastoral tasks. There is little evidence that cities came into being anywhere earlier than 4000 BC. Even the great cities of the ancient and medieval world in Europe and Asia contained only a small percentage of the population. Until well into the present century, rural life and the rural pursuits of farming and tending cattle predominated. As late as 1920 more Americans lived in the countryside of the United States of America than lived in cities. In 1900 Britain and Belgium, for example, were quite exceptional communities because there more people lived in cities than in the rural areas.

The purpose of emphasising the predominance of food production over most of human history is to draw attention to the simplicity of life which our predecessors, until only a few generations ago, experienced. They lived in the presence of the natural necessities and were directly conscious of them in a way which we are not. Most of our ancestors used simple tools. If one visits the museum attached to the Duomo, the great cathedral in Florence, there one can see the tools used by the architect, Brunelleschi, and his fellow-workmen, to build the immense, solid and beautiful church, St Maria del Fiore. These are few in number and simple in design and construction; vastly different to the array of engines, hoists, cranes and mixers used in the construction of modern buildings.

We men and women of the late twentieth century live in circumstances very different from those of our ancestors. This difference is mainly due to the differences in the tools which we use to produce the food, shelter, clothing, transport, communication and amusements necessary for life. These tools have immensely increased human productivity. So complicated have they become that tools produce tools, and some of them can, without too much exaggeration, be said to think for themselves.

As a result of the rapidly accelerating advances in technology and toolmaking it is easy to lose sight of the natural necessities so evident to our ancestors, most of whom lived short, hardworking lives. Yet these natural necessities are still with us, and frequently in a more acute and puzzling form than ever before. We cannot neglect the relationship of technology and politics. Indeed, the consequences of technological development are at the very heart of modern politics in a way which Robinson Crusoe or his contemporaries would have found strange and inexplicable.

The increase in scientific knowledge of the natural world—the heavens and all that therein is—and the know-how which grows out of scientific knowledge and technological advance appears as a great blessing to mankind. Our lives may be still brutish in many ways, but they are no longer short. Even in the poorest countries people live longer than they used to do fifty years ago, and in countries like Japan, for example, which have 'modernised' in a very impressive way, the length of life of the people has almost doubled in half a century. Even in China, which is still a backward and poor community with very low standards of living, there has been a 'population explosion' so dangerous that the Communist government has inaugurated a very severe regime of population control. The reasons for the rapid expansion of the population of the world, which began in the eighteenth century and has accelerated rapidly since World War II, are largely the improvements in food production and in health care. Famine—the acute shortage of food—is no longer a danger everywhere as it once was. It occurs nowadays in very few communities, and then usually as a result of social and political breakdown, and not because there is an absolute lack of food in the world as a whole. In fact, nowadays famines, when they occur, develop even though there are large surpluses of food in some parts of the world and the means of quickly transporting it to areas where there are shortages.

The same may be said of disease. Men and women nowadays—and especially in technologically advanced communities—generally die of old age or genetic and cellular imperfections. Smallpox, which was once a terrible killer disease, no longer exists, and diseases like tubercolosis, measles, and cholera, which used to kill millions of all ages, are now much diminished and have all but disappeared in large parts of the world. Even the loss of life by political disease, i.e. in wars, genocidal and class slaughters, like the murder of several million Jews and gypsies in Germany in the 1940s and the murder of the élite, the kulaks and enemies of the state in the Soviet Union between 1917 and 1952, has not checked the growth of population.

Accompanying the growth in population has been a great growth in the consumption of goods and services. Although the opportunity to eat more, have more leisure, travel more and have more and more material possessions is not equal for all, vast masses of people in the world do lead materially better lives than our grandfathers and grandmothers. Communications are so much improved by electronic technology that today we are said to live in a global village where everyone knows almost instantly what is happening on the other side of the earth.

All this may be counted as a blessing which flows from technology and scientific knowledge, but there is another aspect of technology and science which is far from benign and is much more a terrible problem than a welcome blessing.

If we think of war as a political disease—as a failure to co-operate for the good of all—technological advance has vastly increased the killing power of weapons. Indeed, it is now possible as a result of technological advance in the manufacture of atomic explosives, and the means of their delivery at enemies, to contemplate the destruction in a few hours or a few days of more lives and property than the severest famines or the worst plagues which our ancestors encountered. Furthermore, technological change has a serious destabilising effect upon society. Robots replace men and women at work. Electronic devices replace clerical and administrative staffs. The men and women who understand modern technology and know how to build and service robots, computers and electronic communications systems increasingly do the work of society and those who lack the education, the intelligence or the character to master the use of the new tools with which our scientists and engineers provide us are left with nothing to do.

Finally, there is another aspect of technology and improved material standards of life which must be considered. For the past 200 years we have been extracting from the earth's mantle increasing amounts of coal, oil and gas which we burn in furnaces, power-generating stations, motor vehicles and aircraft. As a result of this burning, there is discharged into the earth's atmospheric envelope increasing quantities of carbon dioxide and other gases. Impartially viewed, as it might be by an indifferent but scientifically knowledgeable God, this process looks like a slow fire converting the earth into a cinder which will only extinguish itself when the atmospheric gases make burning no longer possible and/or the fuel supply is exhausted. The active agency in this burning process is the human race. The observing God may well say to Himself, 'Are these human beings capable of making a decision in this matter of their fate? Will they find a solution to their problem of survival? I have promised them eternal life, but on conditions which maybe they have forgotten or do not believe or wish simply to ignore. We shall see.'

Thus it is that the problem of our survival is still with us: not the simple politics of survival which Robinson Crusoe faced on his island, but the complex politics of a technologically sophisticated world. Nonetheless we, like Robinson Crusoe or our ancestors living in simple agricultural societies, have to make decisions and choices about what we are going to do and how we are going to do it. That is what politics is about.

Politics is not just about parliaments, parties, congresses, politicians, foreign affairs, voting, conquest of power and ideologies. These are particular aspects of politics. Parliament, for example, is not there just to be studied or visited. The United Nations is not a world theatre where nations and their leaders dramatise themselves and engage in propaganda on their own behalf. Parliaments, party congresses, the United Nations, Councils of Ministers, National Assemblies are gatherings where choices are made, and these choices may be very particular choices about small concerns but they can also determine the fate of millions and even the human race as a whole.

It seems evident to a reasonable person that the political and moral problems of human kind have a constant character, although they manifest themselves differently from age to age. It is not surprising that we are still discussing topics like freedom, justice and equality as Plato, Socrates and Aristotle did in ancient Greece over 2000 years ago. Our natural necessities are always with us, and they are always a limitation defining our freedom, like the rules which determine what a player and a team may or may not do when playing a game of football.

Politics is not, however, a game. Men and women have made the rules of football, for example, and rules enable people to play this game or any game we care to name. The underlying rules of politics have not been made up by men and women. They are prescribed by nature. They can be broken, but both experience and reason show that breaking them can and will produce terrible, and even fatal, consequences. Men and women can understand the laws of nature, but they cannot suspend or transcend them. Men and women are not gods. This truth is the beginning of politics.

Paradoxically, it may be said that politics is not a game, but that the best hope of men and women in the presence of their political problems is to convert politics into a game, i.e. an activity defined by rules. In fact that is what men and women have done since time immemorial, and not only men and women but all living beings. They have created laws and customs that enable them to co-operate in their work, in the reproduction of their kind, in the protection and the education of their offspring and in the maintenance and extension of their stock of natural resources.

Laws and customs are positively regarded and sometimes revered as sacred because of the underlying knowledge that the alternative to laws and customs is, on the least reckoning, inconvenience and, at the worst, chaos in which every man is for himself and the devil takes the hindmost; sometimes, everyone else as well.

Albert Einstein, the great physicist, whose discoveries were an important factor in the development of modern nuclear science, once said that politics is a much more difficult subject than physics. He was right, not because politics is more intellectually demanding than physics, but because politics is morally demanding; because it requires the understanding of men and women who are less uniform in their behaviour than atoms or sub-atomic particles, and each of whom has an independent will and character, which can be called by the old-fashioned word, a soul.

2 Politics is about Protection and Order in Society

All societies, from the most simple and primitive to the largest and most complicated, are distinguished by order. Order involves behaviour on the part of individuals and groups of individuals which enable them to live together and work together without destroying or injuring each other.

Let us consider an example of order and its importance to individuals: the driving of motor cars. Millions of people drive motor vehicles. At the wheel of such a vehicle the power of a person is vastly greater than his or her individual strength. Every driver has under his or her control the means of instantaneous death for others and themselves. Yet millions of people drive motor vehicles all their lives without killing anyone or being killed, and often without doing significant damage to their vehicles or those of others. When two vehicles travelling in opposite directions along a country road pass each other at 40 miles an hour, both drivers are in the presence of instantaneous death. Only with extreme rarity does death occur. Why not? Because both drivers are kind, good people who would never kill anyone? Because they are extremely quick-witted and wary? Because they are lucky? Because they fear death? No. Both pass each other without fear or thought because both drivers follow a pattern of behaviour—or an order—which the laws of their country oblige them to learn, so that it has become as much unconscious and natural to them as breathing or digesting food. They are saved from destruction and enabled to travel safely and vastly more quickly than they would ever do on foot, not only because they possess a motor vehicle but because they follow an order which governs or gives a fixed pattern to their behaviour.

Order is not something invented by modern men and women who drive motor cars and live in huge cities. The Nuer, for example, are a people who live near the White Nile in the border lands of Uganda and the Sudan. When first systematically observed by anthropologists early in this century they numbered approximately 200,000. They lived in great simplicity, and on that account were called a primitive people.

They devoted their energies principally to herding cattle and raising cereal crops in difficult country where annual flooding obliged them to move their cattle to high ground. Those who observed them could discern little or no evidence among the Nuer of what we could call government or lawmaking. There could be observed, however, among them order and patterns of behaviour which enabled these people to live in reasonable peace with one another in spite of the many causes which existed for disputes about the movement and grazing of cattle. One Nuer might kill another Nuer in the course of a dispute, but the Nuer people had developed modes of behaviour and procedures which prevented even the gravest offences committed by one against another from exploding into war between families or groups of families.

The evidence gathered by anthropologists and historians suggests strongly, though it does not prove conclusively, that no society at any time or in any place has ever existed without order, i.e. patterns of human behaviour which enable individuals to co-operate together for the achievement of purposes prescribed to them by the circumstances in which they find themselves, whether they be Nuer herdsmen or modern motorists.

How does order come about and how is it maintained? These are questions not easy to answer in a way which covers all cases. It would appear that in the remote past and in simple societies, of which we have knowledge, order and custom were the same. People behaved as they did because that is the way people behaved; as their neighbours behaved or their parents and grandparents and ancestors before them had behaved; often because that is how God or the gods, or the resident spirits, wanted them to behave. Individuals who refused, or were unable to behave in accordance with custom, were punished or killed or exiled, or regarded as mad, or subjected to special treatment or even revered as extraordinary beings with magical or incomprehensible powers. No matter how those who did not follow accepted customs were treated, the effect, if not the purpose of the treatment, tended always to be the preservation of the customs which the obstinate individual (who might be called a 'drop-out') refused or failed to observe.

It is safe to say that the order observable in the societies in which we live in the late twentieth century is not based on customs. Customs there are, and sometimes the unconscious power of custom is greater than we imagine in modern societies, but in all the main human activities which require a pattern of behaviour on the part of the individuals or groups of individuals, the pattern observed in behaviour is based on law, not on custom. To a Nuer driving his cattle from wet land to dry, his behaviour towards other Nuer doing what he is doing was customary and not a matter of premeditation or thought. To a modern motorist his behaviour as a driver on a public highway is no more premeditated than a Nuer driving his cattle. The modern driver behaves as he or she does without premeditation and according to the behaviour patterns they have learned, which are the same as those of their parents or their grandparents. The modern motorist behaves, however, in accordance with a Highway Code whose authority is derived from an act by a lawmaking body, and its provisions are enforced by police appointed by the executive arm of government. The vast majority of motorists obey approximately the Highway Code of their country, not because there are police to enforce the code but because they do not wish to kill or maim themselves nor, what is often a more important consideration, damage their motor cars. The law reinforces this view of motorists' self-interest, for if, in the event of an accident, it can be shown that the accident can be attributed to breaking the Highway Code, the costs to the offender are greatly increased, both in terms of punishment as a criminal act and/or increased civil damages and increased insurance premiums.

There is another angle from which laws as distinct from customs must be examined. Laws are written, and they are the result of the conscious premeditation of those who write them down and enforce them. The Nuer could not read and write. No code prescribed what a Nuer should do if he suffered a wrong at the hands of another Nuer. Custom required that a man's kinsmen take joint action to avenge a death or extract compensation for an injury; but the kinsmen of both the offenders and the victim knew that vengeance or the extraction of compensation by force meant war. The Nuer avoided this possibility, or greatly diminished it in the common interest, by two means: the payment of compensation and the mediatory activity of 'the leopard-skin chief'. This chief had no power, but he might *in extremis* pronounce a curse on the parties. Nuer society was full of antagonisms, disputes and killing, but their customs involved behaviour which restrained them from extremes of social disorder, and this without the existence of a strong third force capable of enforcing rules of behaviour.

Something similar seems to have existed among the Anglo–Saxons who established themselves in Britain in the fifth and sixth centuries. They had a custom of compensating for injuries, including death, by money payments. There was, in fact, a sort of price list: one shilling for a finger-nail and 10 shillings for a big toe. We know this because when Christianity was established in Kent by St Augustine and some of the people, mainly churchmen, began to read and write, Aethelberht, the King of Kent, proclaimed his dooms, or laws, early in the seventh century AD. The dooms of the king were written statements of customs already established for the preservation of public order. There may have been something new in them inasmuch as the compensation to be paid for thefts from clergymen was very heavy: twelve times the value of the property stolen from a bishop, nine times from a priest and six times from a deacon. But much in the dooms of Aethelberht seems to have been a restatement in written form of established practice, e.g .the kinsmen of a murdered man could claim 100 shillings from the murderers; and a freeman who bound himself in service to another was entitled to 20 shillings; and anyone who broke into a farm surrounded by a hedge paid 6 shillings.

All of this presupposes that the King of Kent could enforce the laws he proclaimed. This seems to have been the case, because the compensation extracted from anyone who misbehaved in the King's presence was very heavy, e.g. 50 shillings to the King for killing anyone in his presence on top of the wergeld, or compensation payable to the dead man's kinsmen. Aethelberht's regime in Kent seems, however, to have been much milder than that of a not-too-distant neighbour of the Nuer, the Buganda, whom the British explorer, Speke, visited in the 1860s. The Kabaka of Buganda punished misbehaviour in his presence with terrible and arbitrary cruelty, much as Idi Amin in the 1970s in Uganda. Like Amin, the Kabaka ruled by terror. By contrast, Aethelberht seems to have had a policy of increasing his resources by fining people who misbehaved, and in this way was better able to pay the armed retainers who sustained his power.

Although there is evidence that in other times and other places order has existed without government, the existence of a stable order in society without the presence of a sovereign authority capable of making laws and enforcing them is seldom or never found nowadays, nor often in the history of civilised, as distinct from primitive, societies in the past.

Writing in the seventeenth century during the years of civil war which divided English society as it has never been divided since, the philosopher, Thomas Hobbes, came to a conclusion which it is very difficult to challenge. He argued that

It is manifest, that during the time men live without a common power to keep them all in awe, they are in that condition which is called war; and such a war, as is of every man, against every man ... Whatsoever there is consequent to a time of war, where every man is enemy to every man; the same is consequent to the time, wherein men live without other security, than what their own strength and their own invention shall furnish them withall. In such condition, there is no place for industry; because the fruit thereof is uncertain: and consequently no culture on earth; no navigation,

Thomas Hobbes (1588–1679)

nor use of any commodities that can be imported by sea; no commodious building; no instruments of moving and removing such things as require much force; no knowledge of the force of the earth; no account of time; no acts; no letters; no society; and which is worst of all, continual fear, and danger of violent death; and the life of man, solitary, poor, nasty, brutish and short.

In Hobbes' view any government is better than no government. Without government there is no law, and no means of enforcing law. This is not a very popular view in democratic societies. In all societies where there is even moderate freedom of expression, there are frequently to be found numbers of people who individually or collectively think the government they have ought to be replaced by one more to their taste. Frequently this is not just a matter of believing that the ins ought to be out, and the outs in; it is a belief that the whole apparatus of government ought to be scrapped and replaced by something revolutionary and new. It is by no means the case that everyone shares Hobbes' view that any government is better than no government.

Experience shows, however, that very frequently those who think that anything is bound to be better than the government that exists in their society, end up with governments which are larger and more powerful than those they have overthrown. The reason for this is quite simple to discover. The overthrow of a government creates conditions much resembling the state of affairs which Hobbes called war. This state is so horrible that more and not less, and stronger not weaker, government becomes acceptable to society; and, acceptable or not, that is what in fact happens. The victory of the Parliamentary forces in the English Civil War, the French Revolution which destroyed the absolute monarchy in France and the Russian Revolution which ended government by the Autocrat of all the Russias did not result in less government or no government. In every case governments emerged much stronger and with greater power over the lives of the governed than had the regimes overthrown by the malcontents. In our own day the overthrow of Batista, by Fidel Castro, in Cuba has not led to less or better government, but more and worse government. This has been equally true in Cambodia and Iran. It is likewise evident that the strenuous and successful political movements which ended the British, French and Dutch Empires after World War II have not produced less and better governments in the liberated communities. In the matter of government it seems to be the case that beyond a certain point more means worse.

It is necessary, therefore, to investigate the arguments of Hobbes in support of political sovereignty as a solution to the 'order problem', which means the maintenance of peace and security in place of the alternative of war and insecurity.

Hobbes' method of argument is not one much favoured by modern social scientists. To begin with, he invites his readers to consider a state of nature which has never existed. If by state of nature one means the condition in which the human race existed at some time in the past when men and women lived lives of great simplicity, used few tools and were comparatively few in number, it would be difficult to make any significant general statements about the state of nature. Hobbes' references to the Indians of North America suggest that he may have had in mind real primitive people in a state of nature, but as his argument was developed, it is clear that Hobbes' state of nature is an imaginative construction, the purpose of which is to describe the essential characteristics of human beings, natural to them and 'such as experience has found true . . .'

Hobbes' natural man has two general capacities: to think and to want or desire. Thinking is a matter of taking into the brain the sights, sounds, smells, tastes and touch where these are stored as images, some of which are retained and others are noticed but not retained. The brain scans these images and draws conclusions about the relationship among images by a process of addition and subtraction. In several respects Hobbes, in his account of mental activity, anticipated by three centuries the 'mental' processes of computers. Of course, Hobbes acknowledged that the human mind does not function always as he described it in principle. Human beings can, for example, think about words rather than about what we call sense data, and words may not have precise meanings relating to the data supplied by the senses. Then confusion supervenes and nonsense is generated. Hobbes would have said of the mind what many have observed about computers: 'If you put garbage in you get garbage out.'

Nonetheless, man takes in sense data, reflects upon these data and draws conclusions about the relations among the sights, sounds, smells, taste and touch which he or she experiences. This information and its analysis Hobbes called science, which is 'the knowledge of consequences, and dependence of one fact upon another'.

Hobbes made a very sharp division between what men know and what they do. What they do is determined by desire or aversion, i.e. by positive and negative impulses.

Desires and aversions are the essence of life,

> . . . the felicity of this life consisteth not in the repose of a mind satisfied. For there is no such *finis ultimus*, utmost aim or *summum bonum*, greatest

good, as is spoken of in the books of the old moral philosophers. Nor can a man any more live, whose desires are at an end, than he whose senses and imagination are at a stand. Felicity is a continual progress of the desire, from one object to another; the attaining of the former being but the way to the latter. The cause whereof is, that the object of a man's desire, is not to enjoy once only, and for an instant of time; but to assure for ever, the way to his future desire . . .

Power, Hobbes defines as the capacity to satisfy desire. All men and women have power. Men and women differ in their powers, but the differences are not so great that 'one man can therefore claim to himself any benefit, to which another may not pretend, as well as he. For the strength of body of the weakest has strength to kill the strongest, either by secret machinations, or by confederacy with others, that are in the same danger with himself.'

Hobbes summed up the logic of his description of a man as a 'felicity-seeking animal' bent on maximising the satisfaction of his desires and minimising his aversions in these words:

So that in the first place, I put for a general inclination of all mankind, a perpetual and restless desire of power which ceaseth only in death. And the cause of this, is not always that a man hopes for a more intensive delight, than he has already aspired to; or that he cannot be content with a more moderate power; but because he cannot assure the power and means to live well, which he hath present, without the acquisition of more . . .

In other words, he wants good pay now and a good pension and he wants it indexed or in some way preserved against inflation. Or maybe he wants the control of central Asia, and to assure the future he must control Afghanistan and then maybe Pakistan and then India and then and then to the end of the world.

The equality of individuals and their unlimited desires produce a politically explosive circumstance which Hobbes called war. It was in this sense that Hobbes believed the war of man against man to be a natural fact and a problem which man is obliged to solve. Desire causes war and war makes the satisfaction of desire impossible. Of course there may be people who delight in life which is 'poor, brutish and short', but this is not the natural desire of everyone any more than a desire for, say, pickled onions is a universal and general desire. For the majority, war is a problem which they desire to solve, because they have many other competing desires.

Hobbes explains the 'order problem' thus:

> The final cause, end, or design of men, who naturally love liberty, and
> dominion over others, in the introduction of that restraint upon themselves,
> in which we see them live in commonwealths, is the foresight of their own
> preservation and of a more contented life thereby . . . For the laws of nature,
> as justice, equality, modesty, mercy, and, in turn, doing to others as we
> would be done to, of themselves without the terror of a power to cause them
> to be observed, are contrary to our natural passions, that carry us to partiality,
> pride, revenge, and the like. And covenants, without the sword, are but
> words, and of no strength to secure man at all . . .

Men and women can and do use their reasoning power to work out rules
of conduct and institutions which should enable them to live in peace
with one another, as we once established a League of Nations and then
a United Nations Organisation. We have, for example, widely
accepted the simple rule of life laid down by Jesus Christ: '. . .
Whatsoever ye would that men should do to you, do ye even so unto
them; this is the law . . .' But experience shows that we do not follow the
rules which God and reason tells us is the way to peace and fulfilment.
Hobbes sought a practical solution: the sovereign, 'the terror of some
power to cause them to be observed'.

A sovereign or ruler is created by an act of will, by a contract or
covenant which consists of delivering up to one person or a body of
persons all the natural rights of individuals to life and liberty and the
satisfaction of their desires in return for the preservation of peace and
order. Hobbes' argument is severely logical. The individual cannot
enjoy life, and liberty in a state of nature, which is a state of war.
Therefore, he must deliver up life and liberty to a power that can
guarantee him peace and order. He will enjoy a new liberty, not defined
by himself but by the sovereign. The only obligation of the sovereign to
his subjects is the preservation of peace and order, and the failure to do
so is the only circumstance which releases individuals from their
obligation to obey the sovereign. Hobbes goes further, and argues that
the obedience which a subject owes to the sovereign is an expression of
his own will inasmuch as the subject has agreed by a covenant or
contract to create the sovereign in order to escape from the natural condition of war.

When or where did men and women ever gather together to make a
convenant establishing a sovereign? When Hobbes published the
Leviathan in 1650, there were already in existence several sovereigns
whose regimes answered in many respects to Hobbes' description of
one. They determined the religious beliefs of their subjects. They
censored books. They controlled universities. They defined crimes and
punished them. They maintained laws defining property rights. They
controlled trade and markets. They conscripted soldiers for service in

their armed forces. They levied taxes. They appointed judges. They were the fountains of honour in the communities they governed. They made war on other sovereigns and they made peace. Five years after the appearance of the *Leviathan* in print, the King of France, Louis XIV, declared to the Parlement de Paris, *L'État c'est Moi*. I am the state. He was not boasting.

The most popular explanation or justification for the power of the sovereign, and the one most sovereigns favoured, was religious. God ordained that men and women should be ruled as they were. God required obedience to the powers that be. In his letter to the Christians in Rome St Paul laid down the line about obedience to the state: 'Let every soul be subject unto the higher power. For there is no power but of God: the powers that be are ordained of God. Whatsoever therefore resisteth the power, resisteth the ordinance of God, and they that resist shall receive to themselves damnation.' The only English sovereign much given to theorising about his position, James I, favoured this view of his authority. God gave it to him.

Hobbes, however, believed that there was too much disagreement about religious truth to provide a sure intellectual foundation for anything as important as the sovereign. Religion in his day was the cause of war, not peace. Only two years before the publication of *Leviathan* the princes and bishops of Germany, the Emperor of the Holy Roman Empire, the kings of Spain, France and Sweden and the government of the United Provinces of the Netherlands had signed the Treaty of Westphalia, which brought to an end thirty years of devastating war in which religion had been an important point of dispute.

The sovereign was not the creature of God, but of the people. But what about the absolute monarchy of, say, Louis XIV in France? Hobbes argued that governments are instituted by conquest or by agreement. If one accepted the rule of a conqueror in order to obtain peace and order, one implicitly accepted all the consequences of the conquerors' authority which can be summed up in the word 'obedience'. In England, when Hobbes was writing and thinking men were engaged in a debate about the power of the Crown; they debated with arms in their hands, and found a resolution of their differences on the battle-field. After Oliver Cromwell had defeated the Royalists at the Battle of Worcester, he did not at first know whether the victory was tactical, i.e. a triumph in a war which would continue, or a total victory from which the Royalists could not recover. In reporting to Parliament, Cromwell stated that he did not yet know whether his victory was a mercy or a crowning mercy. As it turned out, his intelligence officers were able to assure him that he had won a crowning mercy.

In so describing his victory Cromwell used a traditional argument, that God's will in politics manifests itself in military success. Hobbes, on the other hand, regarded military success as only one factor in politics. The sovereign required strength, of course, but the sovereign's authority and power must be based on the assent of the governed. They must obey government, because obedience is in their ultimate interest. In this respect Hobbes was a democrat.

For Hobbes, however, the only liberty which the subject can have is the right to do those things about which the law or the orders of the sovereign are silent. In this respect he is, in spite of being dead for more than three centuries, thoroughly modern. There is very little in our world which is not governed by rules prescribed by the state. In many respects the government of the USSR most resembles the sovereign described and advocated by Hobbes. Hobbes, for example, allows no place for private conscience or private judgement : '. . .the law is the public conscience, by which he hath already undertaken to be guided. Otherwise, in such diversity, as there is of private conscience, which are but private opinions, the commonwealth must needs be distracted, and no man dare obey the sovereign power, further than it shall seem good in his own eyes.' Stalin and his successors could not have put it better.

Yet there is in Hobbes' arguments about sovereign authority something which all students must seriously consider. Order and peace are necessities of human life, and there is a price which individuals must pay for their maintenance. Is that price the surrender totally of the liberty and conscience of individuals?

With Hobbes the presumption is that the government is always right in much the same way as the Central Committee of the Communist Party of the USSR insists that it is always right. But is not the Queen-in-Parliament always right for British subjects? It is very seldom that everyone thinks so. Indeed, it is hard to recall when Parliament was ever unanimous in its decisions, and it is inconceivable that all the British people are unanimous about a decision of the Queen-in-Parliament. Nonetheless when the Queen-in-Parliament has made a law, that is the rule for the British community, just as much as a law made by the Supreme Soviet is a law for the people of the USSR. The final authority—the sovereign—has spoken, and that is that.

We know from experience that this is so, but we also know that the interest of government and the interest of the subjects, or some of them, is not always identical. There are people whose character is such that what they are told to do by authority is always what is right to do, is what they want to do and is what they believe it is in their interest to do. We know further from the experience of history that policies embarked upon by governments, often with wide support, have turned out to be wrong on any reckoning, i.e. that they have not achieved the objectives which the authors of the policies promised or expected. Those people, who are always sceptical critics of what governments do, seem to be right in their judgements as often as those who always support what governments do. There seems to be something both right and wrong in Hobbes' argument about the infallibility of the sovereign.

We have chosen the Highway Code as an example of a set of rules—an order—which the vast majority of people who drive motor vehicles obey automatically and which, for practical purposes, no-one questions. As a set of authoritative rules, which prevent men and women from destroying themselves and their property, and enable them to achieve the satisfaction of all of them, the Highway Code promulgated and maintained by the sovereign is a very good example of the work of government as imagined by Hobbes. Anyone who in Britain, for example, defied the basic rule that one drives on the left on a public road would soon either be dead, injured or arrested. The same would be true for anyone on the continents of Europe or North America who insisted on driving on the left. The success of the Highway Code as a system of order depends on the obedience of the drivers, and this obedience is the practice of the overwhelming majority of drivers; otherwise there would be chaos on the roads.

Let us consider how this miracle of order is achieved and enquire whether or not the miracle has relevance to other human activities in addition to the driving of motor vehicles. We must keep in mind Hobbes' assumptions that the behaviour of individuals is caused by their desires; that the realisation of their desires depends on their power, and that all are so nearly equal in power that anyone can mortally injure anyone of the others. A half-horsepower three-wheeler can destroy a Rolls-Royce. Hobbes might argue that the Highway Code works because each driver is terrified of the consequences of breaching its provisions, and this terror is personified by the police, who are the instruments of the sovereign.

Anyone who believes this will believe anything. The source of terror is the knowledge of the facts of life and death on the public highway. However, this bothers only the very nervous. The Highway Code works with a high rate of success, mainly because in their situation as drivers, men and women have simple and similar desires. They all want to get from A to B and to do so in a motor vehicle. Both their desires and their power are such that each individual is in a potentially deadly situation. But they all have the same simple desires and a simple mode of procedure for realising them. Simplicity of desires and known procedures for realising them produce social co-operation, harmony and peace. The drivers of motor vehicles resemble the Nuer driving their cattle from wet land to dry. Similarity of goals and established procedures for their realisation preserve the peace and make social co-operation possible.

Once we move from a consideration of situations where the participants do not have simple desires and the procedures for their realisation are not agreed or are unknown, we can see that the 'order problem' is more complicated. Even so, is Hobbes right in supposing that sovereign authority can pronounce authoritively and effectively? Some will say 'yes'. The sovereign will employ impartial experts who can assess the desires or objections of the participants in an activity; who can decide upon fair and just returns of the activity and can design procedures which will ensure outcomes which may not please everyone, but which will be sufficiently acceptable to avoid conflict.

Others will say 'no'. The sovereign may employ experts and may be able to enforce what they decide, but the experts do not necessarily have all the knowledge to understand a particular activity they are seeking to control; the experts are not necessarily just and disinterested; and indeed it may be argued that justice and fairness are inappropriate ideas for deciding who has what. How can anyone decide what is a fair day's pay for a fair day's work? Or a fair distribution of franchises to search for oil? Or a fair honours list? Or a fair system of education? Not all decisions promulgated and expressed by a sovereign authority are workable or even protective of minimal desires such as the desire for life.

The 'Hobbes' solution' of the problem of order has a central feature common to all governments no matter how they have come into being or what their relationship may be with the communities they govern. Sovereign governments are always small minorities of people in the community who have the power and authority to determine and maintain the rules which order the community. The order created and maintained by Hobbes' sovereign is a product of people who, in relation to the assemblage of individuals always contending one with another, are a third party, like a referee in a football match.

By way of contrast to the 'Hobbes' solution' let us, instead, look at another kind of solution of the order problem; one with a long history and one still very important. The 'Hobbes' solution' supposes a very powerful, active referee who is himself the author of the rules of the game.

Such a supposition little resembles any referee in any game which anyone plays. The referee in a football match is there to enforce rules made elsewhere, often slowly and anonymously by people long dead. The rules which establish a game, and without which a game cannot exist, resemble in principle the laws which define order in society. Sovereign governments may and do make new laws and change old ones, but the total body of laws in any society is always larger, older and more extensive than the laws made even by the most active revolutionary and dictatorial of governments. Because this is so, and has been so for thousands of years, the proposition is not unreasonable that law is the foundation of order and that sovereign governments are but factors in the working of the law and are indeed subordinate to law. The aspiration to create a government of laws and not of men has a long history. The earliest written laws of which we have a substantial record are those of King Hammurabi, who reigned in Babylon from 2123 to 2080 BC, and his code was indebted to an earlier Sumerian code of which we have little knowledge. By comparison, our Magna Carta (AD 1215) is very much a newcomer.

Codes of law spring from the belief that a government of men leaves the subjects of government exposed to the arbitrary will and whims of those with power, whereas a government of laws provides a written, publicly known set of rules binding governors and governed alike. Incorporated in the conception of a government of laws is the idea of constitutional law, i.e. a law governing government; a law which lays down the procedures by which government is created and government operates.

Whence come laws? In a constitutional democracy, such as the United States of America and the German Federal Republic, this question is comparatively easy to answer inasmuch as the legislative authority, such as the Congress or the Bundestag, prescribed by a Constitution, makes the laws, can amend or abolish existing laws and, by implication, is the source of law. But this is a relatively recent development.

In order to understand something of this problem of the source of law, let us consider a short body of law which has been well known in Europe for approximately 1500 years and for much longer by the Jews: the Ten Commandments. The Ten Commandments have never had any legal validity in the law courts of, say, the United States of America nor for many years in the British courts of law. Nonetheless, much British and American law has, until only a few years ago, roughly followed the Ten Commandments in the matter of Sunday observance, family relations and the definition and protection of property.

The discovery of the Ten Commandments is described in the book of Exodus in the Bible, the Old Testament of which is a history of the Jews and a body of stories about various personalities of Jewish history. In the Old Testament fact is mixed with legend and argument, and speculation about human and divine events. The Book of Exodus in particular is an account of the experiences of the Jews while under the control of the sovereign of Egypt, the Pharaoh, and of their prosperity there; of anti-Semitic prejudice leading to an attempted genocide by the Egyptian authorities, and of the migration of the Jews out of Egypt to land beyond the Red Sea. Once free of Egyptian power, the Jews had to devise an order of their own; a law of their own. They were not so vain as to suppose that their escape from slavery and death was all their own work. After all, the Pharaoh and his courtiers, servants and officials claimed that they were divine, a manifestation on earth of a power greater than that of men and women. The Jews had escaped from a divine and mysterious power and they very naturally supposed that this was the work of an even greater power than that which controlled Egypt, where an impressive civilisation had arisen in the Valley of the Nile, and was already thousands of years old. This power, God, had given them life and freedom, and they were grateful for what had happened; but they required order and civilisation in their own affairs. Their leader, Moses, turned to God for guidance and instruction. He went apart from his people into the desert of Sinai, and after communication with the Almighty, reported back, not what he thought, but what God told him. God, Moses told the people, had offered the children of Israel a contract: 'If ye will obey my voice, indeed, and keep my covenant then ye shall be a peculiar treasure unto me above all people: for all the earth is mine.'

In the first place God wanted the Israelites to acknowledge His authority as the creator of everything. They must not attempt to create God themselves by building idols or images or by setting up men supposed to possess His powers. All God offered them were some laws or rules governing their relationship with Him and with one another. These are the Ten Commandments from which all lesser rules derive.

Four of the Commandments concern the relations of the people with God. First, one must acknowledge that there is only one God, and people cannot have other or lesser Gods. Second, God cannot be created by men and women in shape or images or His power attributed to other creatures in the heavens or on earth or in the sea. God is jealous, and He will not tolerate other loyalties. He will punish hard and for many generations. Third, no-one shall speak lightly of God or take His name in vain. Fourth, everyone must set aside one fixed day out of seven free of labour and the other concerns of life, and keep this day holy, a day of rest and a time for expressing reverence for God.

The remaining six Commandments concern behaviour of members of the community to one another. One must honour one's father and mother, and thus acknowledge an intimate secondary organisation of society. No person shall kill another person. No person shall commit adultery, i.e. interfere or disrupt a sexual relationship on which family life is based. No person shall steal, i.e. appropriate the property of another. No person shall lie about a neighbour. And, finally, no-one shall covet another's property or wife or servants or cattle.

The Ten Commandments demand attention because in a very simple way they identify the major factors in social disorder: exaggerated ideas of human power and understanding; violence and lack of respect for the lives of individuals; the appropriation of the products of work by force or fraud; the lack of respect for family life; sexual jealousy and irresponsibility; lying about other people; and jealousy of the possessions and opportunities of others.

As set forth in the Old Testament the history of the Jews does not lead one to the conclusion that law by itself is a solution of the problem of order. The Jews enjoyed great prosperity and preserved their political independence for periods of time; and they also experienced conquest and subjection by others. The prophets who theorised about the experience of the Jewish people always tended to explain that experience in terms of the law: either the Jews forgot God and worshipped idols of their own making or they broke the laws in respect to their social relations, or they did both. If they were invaded and conquered by their neighbours, this was explained as a punishment by God. God dealt harshly with the Jews, but He never said He would do otherwise. They always deserved what they received. They could not blame their fate on anyone but themselves. Their prophets never encouraged them to explain their difficulties in terms of Egyptian or Persian imperialism or upon overpopulation or lack of resources. Indeed, 'the land flowing with milk and honey', which God had promised Moses, was anything but this. Whether it became so depended on the Jews themselves and their character.

This concept of law as expressed in the Ten Commandments has had an extraordinary power inasmuch as it has held the Jews together as a people able to survive in a great variety of circumstances. There is no magic in the Ten Commandments; they are nothing more than applied commonsense in human affairs. This does not mean that they command either respect or obedience by Jews or anyone else, and in modern society they have been almost entirely abandoned. Nonetheless, disobedience still has its penalties, as we daily learn.

The Jews are but an example of peoples in whose affairs law was of decisive importance in their history, and of more account than sovereign authorities of the kind advocated by Hobbes. The barbarian tribesmen of the northern parts of the Eurasian continent who pressed upon the frontiers of the Roman Empire, and eventually infiltrated and destroyed it, were peoples to whom their laws were of very great importance. Perhaps law is not the right word to apply to the 'ordering factor' in the lives of the migratory barbarians of northern Eurasia, for, unlike the Jews of biblical times, the forebears of the Germans, the Franks, the Anglo-Saxons and the Vikings were illiterate and their customs were not stated in writing.

Contact with the Roman and Byzantine Empires and particularly with the Christian churches and their conversion to Christianity had an important consequence for the barbarians, because, as they moved west and south, and settled to an agriculturally based life, reading and writing became an element in their culture and the means of converting their customs into laws. For more than a thousand years, from the collapse of the Roman Empire in the west in the fifth century AD until the emergence and establishment of political authorities on the model described by Hobbes, law was of profound importance to the ordering of society. How was law discovered? What is its source? What are the underlying principles? Who establishes it? How is it enforced? Who is subject to it? Students of law rivalled students of theology, and the study of law, like that of theology, led to the establishment of the great European universities. More than this, law was at the very centre of the politics of the Church and the surrounding communities.

In the Dark and Middle Ages of Europe law had an almost mystic power in the minds of people. There are sound reasons for this. To begin with, laws and obedience to them meant an escape from disorder. Laws, too, were a reassuring expression of customs which were learned by living. The barbarians had customs peculiar to the tribes into which they were divided, and these were the sources of law. Law did not have to be the same for everyone. Furthermore, law could be discovered in the laws of the Roman Empire, which, as people grew in literacy, came to enjoy an intellectual authority even though the power of the Emperor had sunk to nothing. Then there was the Church and the Christian religion. The Christian religion embraced the Jewish concept of law, although the laws given by God did not occupy among the Christians the autonomous importance which they did among the Jews. Nonetheless, law was important, not only as an expression of God's will but as an indispensable means of creating order within the Church, and the community of Christians.

With so many sources of law and the great differences in law from one community to another, the possibility of law turning into its opposite, i.e. chaos, was always present. Indeed, it was just this chaos of laws and authorities that prompted Machiavelli* to ask for a 'new deal' for Italy in the sixteenth century, and Hobbes to argue on behalf of the absolute sovereign in the seventeenth century. In spite of this ever-present possibility, law was for a least a millennium an important element in the growth and development of European society, for it was the means of solving the 'order problem'. Laws rooted in custom, in religion and in the examples of the dead Roman Empire were discovered by kings, princes, priests and rioting peasants and workmen as a means of justifying themselves and of securing acceptance in the community.

In studying the problem of order, students of politics should not allow themselves to believe that there are one, two or three solutions. Solutions are appropriate to circumstances. If there are two things we can we be sure about, change in circumstances is one and the need for order is the other. Dictatorship, which is deducible from the arguments of Hobbes, is a solution of the problem of order, but what kind of solution? Men and women value order, but they value much else. If the maintenance of order involves the denial of some or all of the things which are otherwise valued or hoped for, then the solution of the problem of order itself becomes a problem.

Law, likewise, may be a solution of the order problem, but if the conflict of laws or the maintenance of the laws produce disorder, the solution, too, becomes a problem, and one which men and women will sooner or later have to solve. Laws are no more sacred than government. This obliges us to consider the question of power and authority.

*Niccolo Machiavelli (1469–1527) was a Florentine historian, political philosopher and civil servant. His book, *The Prince*, is a pioneering guide to political practice which assumes that the acquiring and keeping of power is the most important object of political action and that the absolute authority of the sovereign is the key to all else. His views, if not his arguments, anticipated those of Hobbes. To Machiavelli the end justifies the means. Hence the adjective 'Machavellian', which the *Concise Oxford Dictionary* defines as 'unscrupulous, scheming and duplicitous political behaviour'.

3 Politics is about Power and Authority

Anthropologists have observed that among some primitive peoples there is little evidence of centres of coercive power in their societies, i.e. a person or persons who tell people what to do and make them do it. These people, like the Nuer referred to in Chapter 2, maintained order by observing customs, and some of their customs involved procedures for coping with breakdowns of order which manifest themselves as murders, injuries or thefts. Individual Nuers or Nuer families could have engaged in strife, which might have destroyed their society and its members, but they did not do so. This is not because there was a police force or an army to prevent them from pursuing their differences and feuds to the point of war and destruction. At most, the 'leopard-skin chief' cursed the participants in strife. We presume that this had some restraining effect, but at best such curses only reinforced a disposition to follow procedures and to exercise, in the end, the restraint which custom required. The Nuer and many other primitive peoples did not have in their societies agencies which can be identified as sovereign powers of the kind which Hobbes believed to be essential lest society lapse into a natural condition of war and anarchy.

It is possible to suppose that customs, as the 'ordering factor' in society, predominated among our remote ancestors. Not so, however, among our civilised forebears going back a few thousand years. One of the first political scientists of whom we have knowledge was Aristotle, born in 384 BC in the dominions of the King of Macedon and a contemporary of Alexander the Great. His study of politics was in part based upon the observation of how people organised themselves and how they maintained order in the communities in which they lived. These communities were, in the main, located in those parts of Europe, Africa and Asia Minor around the Mediterranean Sea and, particularly, its eastern end.

A general conclusion which one may draw from Aristotle's observations is this. The peoples of whom he had knowledge did not rely solely upon custom to order their societies. They lived in political communities, the common characteristic of which was the presence of sovereign authorities possessing the power to govern. Sovereign authority was not the same in every community, but it was present in all of them. Aristotle observed a state of affairs which we can readily understand. The Greeks, of whom Aristotle was one, were divided into political communities, each of which had a territory, a population and a government, and Aristotle referred also to non-Greek communities, such as Carthage and Egypt. Aristotle's presentation of his material does not suggest that he saw anything novel or recent in the societies he observed. He had a sense of history, and he implied that political change had taken place, but one gains a strong impression that Aristotle regarded the political forms with which he was acquainted as old and well established, and that they were a natural phenomenon resembling biological life, to the study of which he had devoted his early years. For Aristotle the presence in a community of active agencies having the power to make and enforce decisions was normal and something one could study, analyse and describe.

Although there is much in Aristotle which is familiar to us, there is also much that is not. Aristotle observed that political communities consisted of free men. Women and slaves had no part in political life, nor should they have. Furthermore, political communities defined their membership. Although a member of one community might reside in another community, as Aristotle did for some years in Athens, residence did not confer membership and endow an outsider with the rights and duties of a citizen. Aristotle accepted this as an un-challengable fact of life. Furthermore, he did not attempt to discuss political life in terms of a total human community undivided into particular communities, each with their own sovereigns. He could think of Athenians or Thebans, but not of Greeks and, least of all, of human beings, except to say that men are animals capable of justice and therefore of forming political communities.

Aristotle's thinking, as with the thinking of all of us, was shaped by the circumstances of his life and his knowledge of history. Compared with men and women in our world, he lived in a simple society where the population did not grow rapidly, if at all; where the productivity of labour was much the same from generation to generation influenced only by the weather; where the modes of travel on sea and on land were little different to those described by Homer, 500 or more years before he lived and thought about politics. The political communities which Aristotle knew best were city-states like Athens and Sparta. Perhaps he was able to think about politics simply because the political communities of Greece were small and independent, and different from one another, and were not vast, monolithic and mysterious political structures like Persia, against which the Greeks were obliged, from time to time, to fight for the freedom to be themselves.

The purpose of discussing briefly Aristotle's observations and arguments is to emphasise that sovereign government, having power and authority in communities, is very old in human societies, and is probably the mark which most distinguishes civilised from barbarian or primitive societies. Historians, anthropologists and political scientists observing and analysing societies in Europe and elsewhere between the fourth century BC and our own day encounter much that does not fit the model of the state or *polis* as described by Aristotle. However, we can observe a tendency, now fully matured, towards the creation of sovereign authorities which exercise power, make rules or laws and engage in the activities which are associated with the word 'government'.

Sovereigns have power. What is power? The Chinese Communist leader, Mao Tse-tung, who died in 1976, once said 'Political power grows out of the barrel of a gun'. This observation explains in some degree the near-destruction of Chinese civilisation, but it has the merit of a partial truth. Whenever a profound political crisis afflicts a society, those who possess the power of violence, and use it skilfully, win power. The men and women at the trigger-end of a gun have power over those at the other end of it, just as an armed robber has power over an unarmed or outwitted victim. Those at the wrong end of the gun have to submit to the will of those at the other end.

It can be stated as a dogmatic truth of politics that a sovereign must have a monopoly of the power of violence in the community which it governs. No citizen or group of citizens of a state can be allowed to possess the power to challenge or deny the sovereign. That is why no sovereign government can permit the existence of private armies, private police forces or armed partisans to exist within the area of its authority. A sovereign that allows or cannot prevent a breach of its monopoly of the means of violence signs the first clause of its death warrant.

This truth of politics is easily forgotten in communities where the power of the sovereign has long gone unchallenged, and the clash of power-holders which brought it to birth is long in the past. In England and Wales the sovereign has not been challenged in arms for more than three centuries; in Scotland for nearly two and a half centuries. Otherwise in Ireland. Yet the British, long used to talk, debate, elections and policies of compromise, seem to have forgotten the truth so apparent to men like Mao Tse-tung and Fidel Castro. This is especially so of the Americans, whose armed revolution took place more than two centuries ago and whose bloody civil war is nearly a century and a quarter in the past.

This decline among Western democratic states in awareness of one essential ingredient in sovereignty has had tragic consequences. When the British Government came to the conclusion that in the long run one people cannot govern other peoples, they embarked upon the dissolution of the British Empire, and the transfer of sovereignty to communities seeking independence, and even to some who did not. The British Government required that the men and women to whom they transferred sovereignty had the majority support of their communities. In many instances civil wars broke out either before the transfer of sovereignty, as it did in Rhodesia, or soon after, as it did in Nigeria. *Coups d'état* became an endemic phenomenon. The bloodstained soil of what some supposed was once the Garden of Eden, Uganda, is a testimony to the unwisdom of forgetting an essential of sovereignty: a monopoly of violence.

There is, however, more to sovereignty than violence. Already we have used the phrase 'sovereign authority'. The second word is very important, for implicit in it is the idea of obedience to the sovereign for other reasons than fear. Hobbes, for example, argued that people must be terrified of the sovereign's power, but he also argued that people prefer the power of the sovereign to their lot if there were no sovereign to keep the peace and maintain order. They accept the existence and actions of the sovereign because it is an agency for a good which they could not otherwise enjoy. In short, terror is not the reason for obedience to the sovereign. One obeys because it is in one's interest to obey, and only the disobedient need have fear.

The notion of authority is a complex one. It is an obvious fact of life that no-one can know everything. On the other hand, it is evident that some people know more about some things than others do. The men and women who carried out the task of putting a man on the moon obviously knew more about physics, astronomy and engineering than the journalists who compose astrological columns in newspapers or science fiction writers who put their heroes in farther galaxies. In fact the men and women in the National Aeronautics and Space Administration (NASA) of the United States of America know more about space travel than all but a very small number of physicists and engineers elsewhere, and more than the rest of the human race. Their knowledge is very specialised, but in this the men and women in NASA are authorities. They have knowledge and experience of a particular activity which others do not have. Furthermore, the achievement of putting men on the moon reinforces their authority because one does not need a knowledge of physics, astronomy and engineering to recognise that the people in NASA have knowledge which works, and is seen to work.

Expertise in the presence of ignorance is one ingredient in authority. Inasmuch as ignorance always exceeds information—and the more information one has, the more this is evident—it is easy to recognise the limitless possibilities in the generation of authority. We do not know how the universe was created and we do not know whether or when it will cease to be. This is only one kind of ignorance. Anyone or any group of people who can claim knowledge about what is generally unknown and can persuade the ignorant that they have the appropriate knowledge and that this knowledge is important to the ignorant will, at once, have authority.

Authority derives, thus, from what is said and what is believed. The authority of NASA does not present much of a problem because a high percentage of the human race was able to see Neil Armstrong walking on the moon. When we move outside the areas where knowledge can be demonstrated, or where knowledge is used to create things or processes which people can experience as part of their lives, we encounter problems which are not so easy to explain or to solve. When Moses went into the desert and came back with a message from the Creator laying down laws concerning human behaviour, he had a credibility problem. Did the Children of Israel believe him or did they not? He claimed to have knowledge and experience which they did not have. Moses was believed, and so the religion of the Jews was, if not established, at least put on an intellectually clearer footing than heretofore. Henceforward those who studied and understood the Mosaic law, such as the prophets and the rabbis, had an authority among the Israelites which persists down to the present day. It is observable, however, that the degree to which the Children of Israel have deferred to the authority of the law has, and does, vary enormously from total denial to total acceptance.

A sovereign at the trigger-end of a gun may be obeyed, and be able to impose his will on his subjects and to determine the order which prevails in the community where his writ runs. This implies that his subjects do his will but not their own. Fear of death or punishment determines the actions of the subjects. They fear him because of his power, and they obey him on that account. If, however, they obey because they think he is wise or because they believe he can do things they cannot themselves do, or that he has knowledge they do not themselves possess, then their sovereign has not only power but authority. Authority comes, not from fear of death or distress, but from a recognition of one's own ignorance and need for guidance. A sovereign authority is one who has power and is believed to know what is best for his subjects.

This description of a sovereign authority implies that the governors are powerful and well informed, and the governed are weak and ignorant. This is only one way of viewing the matter. Another is to say that the relationship of governor and governed produces a miracle. The weak and the ignorant are made strong and are filled with knowledge by the power and guidance of sovereign authority. Fear of power turns into loyalty and love; ignorance is transformed into information about what to do.

This miracle can be explained. Let us imagine a couple dining in a good restaurant. They know nothing about agriculture, viticulture, butchery or cooking. They are ignorant insofar as the production of the meal, which they are enjoying, is concerned. They are only able to experience the miracle of a good meal because they have either the power or the knowledge or both to command the means of enjoying something about the production of which they are ignorant. The couple are benefiting from a universal circumstance. They are exchanging their powers and/or knowledge for other people's knowledge and capacity to apply it. Of course, they pay their bill with money, but this is nothing more than an intermediary between themselves and the numerous body of people who have produced their meal.

This example suggests a new view of sovereign authority. A sovereign authority possesses knowledge and the means of its application which do not, and perhaps cannot, belong to others. This enables them to provide a service to others which is useful and perhaps indispensable. A sovereign authority, thus, enables individuals to utilise their knowledge and capacities with results which could not be possible if they acted on their own. This, of course, brings us back to Hobbes' original argument about sovereign power as an alternative to chaos.

The view implicit in Hobbes, in the 'gun-barrel' philosophy of Mao Tse-tung and the American movie myths of the 'fastest gun in the West', obscure, because they simplify, the politics of power. Do people come to power and keep power simply because they have guns in their hands and know how to use them more skilfully than others? Do they have authority simply because they know more than others?

Whence comes the sovereign? Whence authority? The sovereign conceived by Hobbes is as much a mystery as the authority of Moses. We can readily see that the sovereign has uses about which arguments can be developed, and the Mosaic law outlines patterns of human behaviour, the usefulness of which can be supported or criticised. But where does sovereign authority come from?

Moses would have had no doubts. Authority comes from the Creator of the Universe, and Moses was a messenger of the Almighty. Mohamet held the same view. King James I, like St Paul, was sure that God ordained the sovereign. Jesus Christ, however, suggested another view, and one which must be considered.

St Mark tells us that certain Pharisees and supporters of the Jewish King, who was maintained on his throne by the Roman Emperor, challenged Jesus to say whether it was lawful to pay taxes to Caesar. Jesus asked them to show him a penny on which was imprinted the image and superscription of the Emperor Tiberius. Then he asked them whose image this was, and they replied, 'Caesar's'. Jesus said, 'Render unto Caesar the things that are Caesar's and unto God the things that are God's'.

Jesus, thus, separated the authority of the sovereign, whose armies controlled Judea and whose tax-gatherers collected tribute from the people, from God whose authority is spiritual and moral. This separation has had profound consequences, many of which the sovereigns of this world have deplored and resisted from that day to this. If we accept this view, we can leave God out of government and address ourselves to the question, how and why are sovereigns created?

Let us begin by asking some practical questions. Sovereigns are people. They may depict themselves as gods or the representatives of God on earth, but, like everyone else, they have to eat. Whence comes their food; their living accommodation; the means of violence of which they have a monopoly? Political power may flow from the barrel of a gun, as Mao Tse-tung said it does, but where did the gun come from?

The Roman Emperor, who ruled a vast empire when Jesus Christ was on earth, had at his disposal a very large and efficient armed force. The Roman legions had to be fed, equipped, paid and provided for. In order to move they required a vast network of roads. They required barracks and, on the frontiers of the empire, great defensive walls and fortifications. They needed ships and harbours. Mao's metaphor of a gun is misleading, because it simplifies the problems which any sovereign has in the exercise of power.

When Aristotle discoursed on government and politics, he assumed that the governors, whether a monarch or tyrant, an aristocracy or an oligarchy, a polity or a democracy,* were served and supplied by

*Aristotle believed that the several forms of government could be classified as either 'good' or 'bad'. Monarchy was government by the man who ruled for the good of his subjects; tyranny was government by one man who served only his own selfish purpose. Aristocracy was government by a few good men who sought to do the best for the

(continued on page 36)

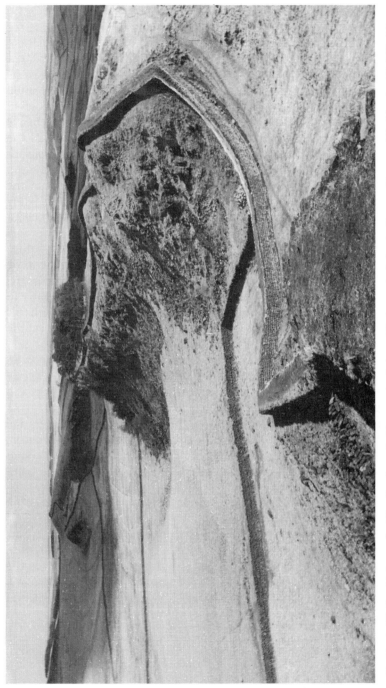

Hadrian's Wall, which runs for 73 miles from the Tyne to the Solway Firth, was built by the Roman Emperor Hadrian in AD 122–30 as a defence against the barbarians from Scotland. It had 17 large forts 5 miles apart and a line of smaller forts (milecastles) each a Roman mile apart. Between each pair of milecastles were two signal towers. Protective ditches ran north and south of the wall

people who had no part in politics and who had no power or authority, i.e. slaves and women. The freemen who made up the polity or democracy of Aristotle were productive people—farmers, shopkeepers and independent craftsmen—but they, too, were heads of households of women and slaves, as well as freemen. One of the Roman heroes was Cincinnatus, a working farmer, who left his plough to lead the Roman army against the enemies of Rome, and he returned to his plough when he had vanquished the Aequi. But Cincinnatus was no more than a reminder of ancient simplicity and anything but the equivalent of the Emperor Tiberius, whose authority Jesus asked his auditors to dissociate from that of God. In fact, when Aristotle and Jesus discussed government and earthly power, the time had long passed when the Greek or Roman political class worked at anything but governing. They produced nothing. They themselves built nothing, but they consumed a very great deal.

Only rich societies can afford sovereigns. What do we mean by rich? In order to understand the word we need to grasp what it means to be poor. It is said of the Duke of Buckingham in the seventeenth and eighteenth centuries that he could ride from his country seat at Stowe to London—forty miles—never leaving his own land. Compared with this Duke, Robinson Crusoe was poor. Yet as a result of his work and the tools and stores he had saved from the wreck of his ship, Crusoe was rich compared with Friday, who became his servant. Riches mean an abundance of things and resources. Poverty is the opposite: a scarcity of things and resources. A rich society has an abundance of things and resources; a poor one the opposite.

When the Nuer were first observed, theirs was a poor society, and they had no government. Compared with them the Buganda were rich, and they had a sovereign in the shape of the Kabaka. Were the Nuer poor because they had no government? Were the Buganda comparatively rich because they had? Perhaps these are not the right questions to ask ourselves. Perhaps one must ask, first, what is the source of riches?

There is one reason why the Nuer were not rich. They lived in a part of Africa where resources—the land, the water and the climate—made life difficult. What they had in the way of goods and shelter was the

community as a whole; oligarchy was a government by a few selfish men who served only their own interest. Polity was government of the people by the people for their own good; democracy was government by the people at the expense of men of property and talent. Because Aristotle, like his teacher Plato, was much concerned with the ideal of perfect government, it is not clear whether Aristotle considered that any living kings were monarchs, not tyrants, or that any aristocracies were not oligarchies or that any polities were not democracies.

product of their work, herding cattle and cultivating pieces of land. The net product of their labours was only sufficient for them to survive and reproduce themselves. It is possible to suppose that they knew their circumstances, and that this is why they had developed customs which restrained their quarrelling with one another and prevented them from spending time and energy in the pursuit of feuds which were destructive of their productive activity. One Nuer might rob another Nuer, but no Nuer or group of Nuer could get themselves into a position where they could live without work by levying a toll on their fellows.

In many parts of the world the conjunction of land, water and climate is more favourable to human beings than that which was the lot of the Nuer. In these areas work yields more wealth, so that more than the minimum of food and shelter necessary for basic needs is produced. Once there is a surplus, a new circumstance emerges, and new possibilities open up. Who receives the surplus? Is it divided in such a way that all have more, or all work less? And even if it is, is there not the possibility that peoples who are less rich, live in less well-endowed parts of the world and are energetic, courageous and ruthless will either seize the resources of the fortunate or appropriate the surpluses for themselves?

The control of the surpluses of a society and their defence against intruders requires an agency with the characteristics and powers which Hobbes attributes to the sovereign. Sovereign authorities need not exist for the good of all. Frequently they exist for the good of some and to the disadvantage of others. Yes, there will be anarchy in the absence of a sovereign, but in their presence there are matters to be considered, of which Hobbes did not take account.

In order to engage in a rational discussion of politics and government, Aristotle put aside the question of slaves and women by attributing to them the natural qualities and characteristics which made them unsuited for citizenship and pieces of property to be used for the advantage of their owners. He thought them insufficiently endowed with the qualities of mind necessary to control their desires and emotions. He endeavoured to reinforce this feeble reasoning and observation with the argument that barbarians are all slaves by nature if they can be caught and subdued. Victory in war carries with it the right to enslave, but in the case of non-barbarians, some account must be taken of the status and quality of those defeated.

There is something in Aristotle's argument about the natural character of slaves and women, but not what Aristotle imagined. Slaves and women were not necessarily less intelligent and less in control of their desires than freemen, but they were in a situation different to that of the freemen. They were workers and producers, and were therefore specialised in their social role. It is difficult for a pregnant women to be a soldier, and a skilled stonemason can have little time for politics or for military exercises. The freeman has time for arms and politics, and the more he can bind slaves and women to providing for his needs, the more free time he has for controlling others and turning them into property for his enjoyment.

There is a simple logic to the economic foundation of politics. All people require food, and nearly all require clothing and shelter of some kind. Food and shelter are products of work. Therefore, all people require work to be done. If the work done provides only enough to feed and shelter all, it follows that all must work. When the work done produces more than is necessary to feed and shelter everyone, everyone need not work. Everyone needs the products of work. This is a constant requirement of a society. The need to work is a variable, once the work arrangements of society yield more than the constant requirements.

How do increases in the productivity of work come about?

The economist Adam Smith (1723–90) gave his famous answer in the first sentence of the first chapter of *The Wealth of Nations*: 'The greatest improvement in the productive powers of labour, and the greater part of the skill, dexterity and judgement with which it is anywhere directed, or applied, seem to have been the effects of the division of labour.' Smith then went on to give an illustration of the miracle of the division of labour. One man on his own cannot produce more than 10 simple straight pins in a day, but ten men each doing a specialised job can produce 4,000 pins a day.

Robinson Crusoe worked on his own, and produced a comfortable life for himself. There was no division of labour on his island. But pause and think about Robinson Crusoe. He had tools and supplies saved from the wreck of his ship. His axes and hammers, his musket, his needles and thread; everything he used was the product of a specialised division of labour in the Europe from which he was cut off. He was not a man alone, as he supposed. He was an individual, of course, but he was also a repository of the experience of a society where there was a well-developed division of labour, and he had, therefore, the knowledge to use the tools he had saved from the disaster which marooned him. His will to survive and his energetic and intelligent employment of tools were his own, but the division of labour was the gift of the society he had left.

There is a consequence of division of labour and the increased productivity which flows therefrom which has been insufficiently considered. Productive work involves specialised attention and time. The activity of productive work likewise produces a kind of personality and consciousness, the sort of disposition which Aristotle noted in slaves and women. They are absorbed in their role in society, and their absorption can be reinforced if there exists in society others who find an advantage in dominating and controlling them.

Just as there develop in society specialists in productive work, there also develop specialists in appropriating the products of work. A successful bandit or robber is a specialist, a person with a certain kind of skill, but he is not a productive specialist. He is a specialised appropriator of the products of work.

The possibility of there being in society specialists in the appropriation of the products of work obliges us to explore sovereignty and power from another angle and at another level. If there was war of all against all, which Hobbes believed the state of nature to be, what was the likely occasion of the war? People can differ and fight for a vast variety of reasons, but one reason does stand out among others as important and constant; the sharing out of the means of work and the products of work. A disposition to quarrel about who gets what is not something recent, nor are solutions of the problem of such quarrelling.

Quarrels about the use of resources such as land for cultivation and for pastures and hunting areas were possibilities among peoples whose work did not yield surpluses of goods beyond the requirements for survival. Such quarrels could only be resolved by reduction in total population. The victors killed some or all of the conquered and used the resources in dispute. When it was discovered, however, that the victors in a quarrel could either levy a tribute—which was only possible if there was a surplus—or that the conquered could be enslaved and put to work for the benefit of the conquerors, new possibilities opened up. The kind of society which Aristotle considered to be natural came into being. A class of consumers now had the upper hand. The division of labour could be improved and extended, the surpluses in society increased. Agrarian civilisation became a possibility, and in the great river valleys of China, India, the Middle East, Egypt and around the Mediterranean civilised societies did come into being. This happened, too, in Mexico and Peru. Sovereign power in a great variety of forms affected the transformation from subsistence societies to civilised communities.

There is more to sovereignty than Hobbes imagined. A contemporary of Hobbes noted this. In his book, *Oceana*, Sir John Harrington observed:

As he [Hobbes] said the law, that without the sword it is but paper; so he might have thought of this sword, that without an hand it is but cold iron. The hand that holdeth the sword is the militia of a nation . . . but an army is a beast that hath a great belly and must be fed; wherefore this will come into what pastures you have, and what pastures you have will come unto the balance of propriety, without which the public sword is but a name or a mere spit-frog (*Oceana*, edited by Liljegrem, p. 49).

Much of history bears witness to the truth of this observation. We need only consider the example of the Roman Empire.

The Romans were originally a tribe, or tribes, of farmers and traders established on the banks of the Tiber river, a few miles from the Mediterranean. They were neighbours of other communities similar to themselves. To protect themselves and their land they were obliged to develop the military and diplomatic arts. For some years, indeed for centuries, they did little more than defend themselves and succeeded only by skilful diplomacy in saving themselves from conquest and enslavement. Eventually they developed a military power and an internal political organisation which enabled them to secure an ascendancy over their neighbours and then the whole of the Italian peninsula. This yielded profit in the form of tribute in money and men for military service—and sometimes slaves for employment as farm labourers and in industrial and mining enterprises. The more land and people they controlled, the more their power grew, until by the time of Christ's birth, the Roman Empire extended from Britain and Lusitania (Portugal) in the west to the borders of Persia in the east and from the Rhine in the north to Upper Egypt and the Sahara Desert in Africa. So long as the Roman sovereign and the Roman Army could find more land to seize and more people to tax or enslave, the Empire flourished. In AD 9 the Roman general, Publius Quinctilius Varus, and three Roman legions were overwhelmed and destroyed by the barbarian Germans in the Teutoberg Forest. Thus the attempt to extend the Empire from the Rhine to the Elbe failed. Henceforward, the Romans were on the defensive. Here and there they had some successes, as they did in Britain in the reign of Claudius and in Dacia in the time of Trajan, but from the reign of the Emperor Augustus, who died in AD 14, the Roman government more and more was concerned with keeping the upper hand inside the Empire and building walls like that of Hadrian in Cumbria and Northumberland to keep out the barbarians.

A vast apparatus was required by the Roman sovereign: to seize lands and peoples; to keep order when they had been seized; to collect tribute and taxes; and to buy off enemies within and without the Empire. In the end the government became a disease from which the Empire perished. All the symptoms of the disease are familiar enough: the debasement of the currency followed by inflation; the control of prices; the control of free labour; the transformation of slaves and poor farmers alike into serfs tied to the land on which they worked; and in

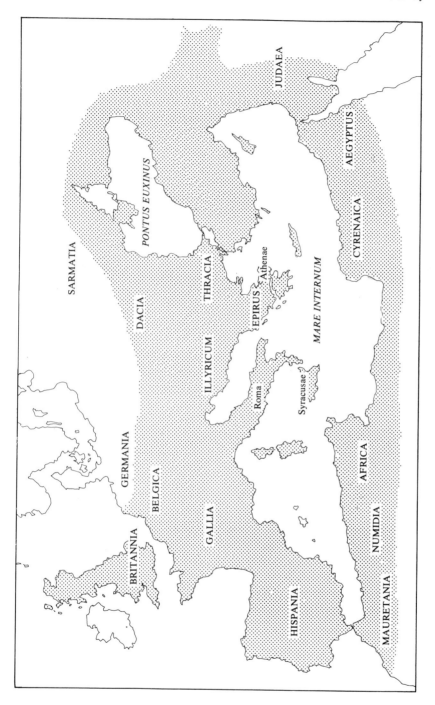

The Roman Empire at its greatest extent in AD 117

parts of the Empire the exhaustion of the soil and the return of the land to desert.

The Roman Empire is the most splendid example of sovereign government as the creator of an exploitive consumer interest; of the antithesis between consumption and productive work. Finally, the soldiers, bureaucrats and politicians of Rome overdid it. They plucked and plundered the poor geese that laid the golden eggs to such a degree that the poor creatures died, or fled, or sought the protection of less rapacious masters. Thus the Empire collapsed in ruins in the West, and Christianity and barbarism prevailed. The things of Caesar's were surely rendered unto him, and grass grew in the Forum and weeds in the imperial palaces. The aqueducts, the baths, the arenas and the circuses fell into ruins and became stone quarries. The subsidised food supplies of the privileged Roman populace were no more. *Sic transit gloria mundi*, and we ask ourselves, can it happen again? Not just the experience of the Roman Empire.

Obviously we require a more searching analysis of the meaning of sovereign power than that provided by Hobbes and all those who believe that political power can solve all problems.

The argument in this chapter tends to suggest that political power determines who gets what in society; that government is theft; that it is the means by which most productive workers are deprived of part of the products of work for the benefit of those specialised in robbing them by enslavement, tribute and taxation. This is a view which cannot be ignored, but it is by no means the whole truth.

The impressive remains of the empire of the ancient Egyptians are, in the main, the pyramids and the temples of the priest–kings: the Pharoahs. We tend to think that these great feats of architecture and engineering testify only to the power and the glory of the Pharoahs and that they used the human power of their society in erecting monuments to their authority and their superstitions. But the Pharoahs were the organisers of great irrigation works which extended the area of land from which the Egyptians won supplies of food much greater than could have been grown and harvested in the marshes and flood plains of the Nile. Without the irrigation systems which controlled the waters of the Nile in Egypt, the people there would probably have been as poor and unproductive as the Nuer who lived much further south and closer to the headwaters of the great river. In short, the government of ancient Egypt was an organiser of production as well as an agency of consumption.

This was also true of the imperial government of China, with its long history stretching from before 1000 BC until the revolution in AD

1911. Irrigation was of great importance for the production of food in the river valleys of China, and the construction, maintenance and administration of the irrigation works were a major responsibility of government.

This brings us to a general point about the relationship of governments to the productive life of communities. Production of goods and services depends upon the division of labour and upon specialisation of skill and the improvement of tools. An indispensable factor in the refinement and expansion of the division of labour is trade between individuals, productive organisations, regions and nations. Trade is facilitated by the use of money, one of the oldest and most important social inventions of the human race. Finally, improvements in the division of labour depend upon saving out of current production in order to make future production possible: what today we call the 'accumulation of capital'.

In its simplest and earliest form, saving out of current production to ensure future production is illustrated by the practice of early agriculture and cattle and sheep farming. Husbandmen, shepherds and cattle herders must save the seedcorn and the breeding stock, otherwise the enterprise fails and the people perish. If, on the other hand, the practice of saving and protecting the seedcorn along with the breeding stock prevails, abundance is possible, and from abundance of food flows other possibilities. Given these natural circumstances, a government is necessary and good if it makes savings for productive purposes possible and secure by preserving peace and order. Another important work of government, depending on circumstances such as existed in Egypt and China, is the organisation and maintenance of aids to production which individuals or families cannot create on their own and which require the mobilisation of labour power on a large scale, for example, irrigation works.

Another positive contribution of governments to productive life in the ancient world was the protection and development of trade. This took two forms: the control of piracy at sea and the safety of merchants travelling by land; and the provision of reliable money.

The Greeks, for example, were a trading people from pre-Homeric times. Money, in some form, is a great convenience to merchants and many widely used commodities have served as money: shells, animal skins and precious stones. However, the most acceptable and widely used money of the ancient world was gold and silver, commodities widely valued, valuable in relation to their weight, their portability, their durability and the fact that they can be hidden with comparative ease and used for ornamental purposes. Money can exist without governments to issue coins, but the coining of money by governments was a great advantage to traders and merchants. A study of coin collections from the ancient world, particularly of the Mediterranean, reveals the great variety and beauty of ancient coinage and the fact that many rulers, otherwise forgotten to history, issued gold and silver coins with which they paid for what they consumed and which they accepted in payment of tribute or taxes. These coins passed from hand to hand in trade, and were or an immense advantage to trading communities, as the Greeks and Phoenicians were. People could at once recognise the reliability of a coin by the effigy of the ruler which it bore, and they could know its weight and purity from looking at it.

Of course, coins were subject to abuse, both by those who issued them and those who used them. Coins could be debased, for example. The government issuing them, when faced with a deficit in their accounts, could add a small proportion of some base and cheaper metal to the gold or silver. The coins looked like the real thing, but were not as valuable as they were supposed to be. A government might be able to pass off such a fraud, but those who received them soon discovered the deception, and their exchange value declined and prices rose. Likewise, those who used coins might shave small quantities of gold or silver off the coins, and thus practise fraud; but again the coins diminished in exchange value as users weighed and tested them. The Roman Emperors were great coiners of money, and at the peak of their power and efficiency their coins were reliable and accepted within a trading community much larger—geographically—than the European Economic Community is at present. This was a great boon to trade and commerce, but in the end the Roman Government could not match its revenues with its expenditure, and it was therefore necessary to resort to the debasement of the currency. Prices rose, and the imperial government attempted to freeze prices, freeze wages and freeze people in their jobs. This, as much as anything else, was a factor in the decline and fall of the Roman Empire, and the destruction of what had, at the height of its power, been an immense and prosperous trading community based upon an extensive division of labour.

Given these facts, it is apparent that governments, then as now, cannot be described as agencies of consumers living at the expense of creative workers, nor as disinterested guardians of producers and traders. Sometimes they are the latter, sometimes the former, and frequently both.

Aristotle believed that the several forms of government which he observed could be classified as good or bad. He was primarily a moralist and, although he had some knowledge of economics, he had an intellectual's disdain for trade and money. He was not able systematically to identify what was bad in the policies and practices of the forms of government which he described. But he was right in supposing that the activities of government are not always benign and not always disastrous.

4 Politics is about Government

The peoples of the world today live in nation-states. There are 175 of them. They have three common characteristics: a territory, a population and a government.

Such territory has a defined boundary, and sometimes these boundaries are more than marked on maps. They are there in the shape of fences, ditches and walls, as well as natural features such as rivers, mountains and seas. The territories of nation states vary enormously in size, from the 189 hectares (467 acres) of Monaco to the 8.65 million square miles (22.4 million square kilometres) of the Union of Soviet Socialist Republics.

Populations, too, vary enormously, from the 30,000 people in Andorra to the 900,000,000 or more who live in the People's Republic of China. Furthermore, the variation of land area in relation to population is enormous. Although Canada has a territory larger than China, the Canadian population is scarcely 2½ per cent that of the Chinese.

Each nation-state has a government, and this government is said to possess sovereign authority over the people in the state's territory. Governments differ greatly in their form and organisation. They have, however, one common characteristic. They are all a minority of the populations they govern, and in most instances a very small minority.

To use the word 'minority' in connection with government implies that a government is made up of people. This is so. But the word 'government' has more than one meaning. Government is an activity: that of exercising power, of making decisions about the order and patterns of activity in society. Governing also embraces the idea of administration—of keeping things going. The operation of the Highway Code, for example, requires administration such as the appointment, pay and supervision of driving examiners, studying the effectiveness of details of the Code itself and so on. Much of the activity of government is devoted to the implementation of decisions about public services or order made in the past, sometimes in the very remote past.

46

In considering government, let us begin with government as people—the minority in the nation-state who tell us what to do and make us do it. This is, perhaps, an unkind, even a brutal, way of describing government, but if we acknowledge that governments have sovereign authority in and over nation-states, this description is apt and true. In any nation-state where this is not true there is trouble and disorder, and life is poor, nasty, brutish and short.

How are these minorities which we call governments drawn from among the population? In the modern world most communities aspire to democracy, even though very few nation-states are by any standard of judgement democratic. The idea of democracy implies that the people govern themselves. But how? Even the 30,000 people who live in Andorra would find it difficult to assemble, decide upon the rules ordering their lives and then proceed to see that all followed the rules. When Aristotle spoke of a polity or a democracy he had in mind self-government in which the citizens, i.e. the male freemen, participated directly in the government of the community, but he was speaking of cities which were small in size and communities in which women and slaves had no voice. Even in these communities self-government meant participation in the selection of officers of government by voting. Practical facts stand in the way of a people governing themselves by collectively making and enforcing decisions about their affairs. Governing is a specialised activity like architecture, pottery-making or farming, and people have to be found who can govern in some way or other.

The most general feature of a democracy is the legal and operationally effective right of every adult in the nation-state to participate in the selection of the personnel of the government and the periodic re-selection of the government. The practice of selection is intended to overcome the impracticality of direct self-government. But there are other aspects of selection to be considered.

If the object of selection were only to find a minority who could take on the task of government one could proceed as is done in selecting juries in Britain, i.e. by random selection from the list of citizens eligible to vote. Why not select a lawmaking body by this means? The names of all citizens could be fed into an Electronic Random Number Indicator (ERNI), and the names of, say, five hundred legislators would emerge. Such a legislature, so chosen, would certainly be democratic. The number of women would be in the neighbourhood of 50 per cent; the proportion of those with less than average incomes would be about the same; the very young and the very old would very likely find some representation. So might racial minorities.

An executive committee to oversee the enforcement of the laws made by the legislature, selected by an Electronic Random Number Indicator, would be similarly democratic in character and so would the selection of a President to hold the supreme power.

It is very unlikely that anyone anywhere would wish to solve the selection problem in this way. It is absurd. But why?

In the first place, a randomly selected legislature would inevitably number in its membership very few with the intelligence, the experience and the willingness to undertake the task of legislation. In the second place a process of random selection would deprive the citizens of an active part in political life. The sovereignty of the people would be yielded to the sovereignty of chance. No bad thing, cynics may say, but the deprivation of the citizen of the right and opportunity to say 'yes' or 'no' in the political process renders meaningless faith in the aspiration we call democracy.

At this point we must pause to consider the idea of democracy. There is nothing natural about democracy, any more than there is about monarchy, or military dictatorship, or the monopoly control of the USSR by the Communist Party. On the other hand, the character of modern society, as compared with that which existed a mere two centuries ago, makes almost inevitable and therefore natural democracy as a widely accepted political myth. One can understand why vast numbers of people, who agree about little in their lives and live in very different circumstances, accept the notion that government of the people by the people, and for the people, is right and proper, even though there is little evidence that a particular government and even any government has that character. Peoples who live in remote deserts and jungles, and who are only a few years away from their primitive past, now know that there are other gods than their gods; that the Judeo–Christian God is not the only god in the universe, and that where there is no God the habits, customs and ways of the Godless are not the only ways of men and women. It is no longer possible to say, as one's ancestors did, that one must obey the government because God ordained it. Which God? What government?

The clearest modern answer to the problem of finding a justification for government, which is not based, like Hobbes' argument, on the practical need for order, was provided by the wandering Swiss intellectual, Jean Jacques Rousseau (1712–78). Government, he maintained, is and must be founded on the General Will. The General Will is not an idea easy to explain. It is something generated by the experience of the people and embraces their customs, habits, religion, interests, prejudices and opinions. Although it is hard to lay hands on the General Will and say this is it, there is no doubt that many great political leaders, some successful and some unsuccessful, have

Jean Jacques Rousseau

displayed remarkable expertise in manipulating this force. The General
Will is the force at the heart of modern nationalism.

It will be at once argued, however, that the great nationalist leaders
such as Hitler or Mussolini were not democrats; they were dictators
and authoritarians. Yes, they were, and national leaders frequently are,
but they were and are democrats. They grounded their power and
authority on the people and upon the General Will, a frequent
constituent of which is hatred and contempt for other peoples who are
not of their language, colour, customs or religion. When one based the
legitimacy of government upon the ordinances of God, it was possible
to conceive of governments doing wrong, but the General Will can
never be wrong, for it is the sole legitimate authority. This is very
flattering to the people, and the source of much misery and failure.

There are, however, factors at work in modern society which
transform and expand the force of the General Will as conceived of by
Rousseau. Although, for example, a strong opinion about racial
superiority may exist in a society and constitute an important element
in the General Will, it is difficult to sustain this prejudice in the face of
evidence that black men sometimes, indeed quite often, prove
themselves faster and more skilful at sports and games than white men.
When Jesse Owens, a black American, won several gold medals at the
Olympic Games in Berlin in 1936, Hitler's rudeness to Owens could
not erase the fact that a black man was superior to white competitors in
feats of athletic dexterity. The fact that Japanese businessmen and
workers are more successful at industrial mass production than
Americans cannot be ignored. Nor is it possible to sustain the notion
that certain accomplishments are the prerogative of privileged people.
William Robertson, a private soldier, rose from the lowest rank in the
British Army to become a Field-Marshal and the Chief of the Imperial
General Staff in World War I. Henry Ford, a mechanic of very limited
education and with no financial resources or backing by financial
interests, built up the largest motor-car manufacturing enterprise in the
world during the first thirty years of the twentieth century. In the middle
years of this century, Ernest Bevin, a mineral-water roundsman,
became the British Foreign Secretary. And, of course, we all know that
the daughter of a grocer in Lincolnshire became the Prime Minister of
the United Kingdom.

Given the fact of social change and flexibility in industrial societies,
and that this fact is widely known and familiar to all, the idea of
democracy is a natural and inevitable one. Who can argue against
democracy, against the notion that all men and women are equal and
equally entitled to participate in political life if they want to? And few
do so argue. Even the most repressive regimes parade themselves as

democratic. Indeed, many governments of this type feel it necessary to incorporate the words 'people' or 'democratic' in the names of their states.

The idea of democracy may be natural to the modern world, but operational, real democracy is not. The benefits and profits of power are too tempting a prize for the seekers and holders of power for them readily to subscribe to and work a political process whose reality and truth involves the possibility that those who hold power can be dismissed from power by the citizens; that power is contingent upon acceptability to a significant proportion of the community and that democracy means, among other things, freedom of the people to learn about, to comment upon and to object to, the behaviour of power-holders

A working democratic political system is one in which all the adult citizens participate in the selection of the government by elections *which the government in office can lose* and *which experience shows governments do lose*. There are not many such political systems in the world. They are to be found in Western Europe, in North America, in Oceania. India, Japan and Sri Lanka are among the few democracies in Asia and Israel is the only democracy in the Middle East; there are few democracies in Africa; Colombia and Venezuela have some of the characteristics of democracy, and Mexico, though a one-party state, has some democratic features. Argentina has once more become a democracy. Elsewhere democracy is a myth or a theme for propaganda and, occasionally, a genuine aspiration, but not a reality.

The impracticability of self-government by all the citizens is one factor in the definition of democracy as a system of government in which the interests and rights of the subjects of government are achieved and protected by the participation of all the citizens in the selection of the personnel of the sovereign authority. Those selected to do the work of government are said to be representative of the citizens. They are said to be responsible if they are answerable or accountable for their actions to the citizens. Thus, democracy, as it is practised in the modern world, is not self-government by the citizens. Government is an activity carried on by selected groups. They are specialists in the activity of governing, but they are not autonomous or separate from the citizens whom they govern. They make and enforce laws and rules; they make and carry out policies; but they are, or are supposed to be, both representative of and responsible to, i.e. answerable to, the citizens for what they do.

A genuinely democratic government, which is both representative and responsible, can never be very much better or very much worse than the citizens which it governs. This is democracy's great drawback, and one of the reasons why it is so easy to suggest alternatives which neglect experience and depend for their appeal on ignorance or flattery, and usually both. Winston Churchill put this very well in the British House of Commons in November 1947, more than two years after his defeat by the Labour Party: 'No-one pretends that democracy is perfect or all-wise. Indeed, it has been said that democracy is the worst form of government except all those other forms that have been tried from time to time.'

The theoretical simplicity and moral attractions of democratic ideas about government conceal the very great difficulty of making them operational in real communities numbering many millions. How do people go about the task of making self-government work?

The United States of America and the United Kingdom of Great Britain and Northern Ireland are examples of large communities with fairly successful democratic forms of government. Although the governments of these nations differ considerably in their structure and ways of working—one is a republic and one is a monarchy—both share a common origin. The practice of representative government is much older than the United States of America, where formal and complete separation from Britain by the American Revolution took place in 1783. Representative government, as it operated in Britain and her American colonies in the eighteenth century, was already a quite distinctive type of government, in terms of the governments which then existed in Europe and Asia; so much so that a French writer on government and politics, Montesquieu, for example, believed the British to be 'free people'.

Representative constitutional government as it existed in Britain at the time of the American Revolution was not, however, uniquely British in origin. When Englishmen of the eighteenth century talked proudly and sometimes boastfully of the British Constitution they meant a body of laws, many of them of great antiquity, which defined the role and determined the activity of the British monarch, the British Parliament, British judges, the British armed forces and the officers of government. British government was constitutional because its structure and the working of the structure were defined by laws, by customs and long-established practices, and it was representative because a Parliament representative of the aristocracy and the Church in the House of Lords, and of the rural interests, as well as the towns and cities, in the House of Commons had a part in the making of laws and an influence on the monarch's appointment of his or her advisers and principal officers of state.

This form of government was not democratic in our sense of the word, and it was not particularly British in origin. If there is any community which can claim to be the Mother of Parliaments, it is to be found in Spain. The King of Leon called together a Cortes in 1188, where representatives of towns joined with noblemen and church representatives in advising the sovereign about laws and policy, and a similar Cortes was assembled in the Kingdom of Castile in 1250. It was not until 1265 that an English nobleman, Simon de Montfort, attempted to force upon the King an institution of a representative character, and he was defeated. But, as frequently happens in politics, the conservative victor in the struggle stole the clothes of the opposition, adopted de Montfort's policies and enjoyed great success. King Edward I, who came to the throne in 1272, won a reputation as a great lawgiver and became the effective founder of Parliament as a part of the English government.

Medieval France, too, developed a representative branch of government—the Estates-General, a body of three chambers: the nobility, the clergy and the commons. It is symptomatic of the differences in political development in Britain and France that the French Estates-General was summoned to meet by the French king in 1614, and never again for 175 years; whereas the attempt of an English king to do without Parliament lasted only eleven years, from 1629 to 1640. In both instances the summoning of a long-suspended representative body was followed in the British case by the English Civil War and in the French by the French Revolution. In both France and England the political commotion of revolution and civil war ended in military dictatorship: of Oliver Cromwell in England and of Napoleon Bonaparte in France.

Military dictatorship in Britain soon ended with the death of Cromwell. One of his most formidable officers, George Monck, who ruled Scotland for Cromwell, decided to make a deal with the Parliamentary politicians and with King Charles II in exile. As a result, the traditional form of British government was restored: a monarchy with an effective representative element in it. When Charles II's brother, James II, attempted to disturb the settlement made with the great interests represented in Parliament, and particularly the Church of England, he lost support in Parliament and in the armed forces, and fled the country. Parliament replaced James II with James' daughter, Mary, and her husband, the Prince of Orange. William and Mary reigned as joint sovereigns.

Before the Civil War the Crown and the Officers of the Crown were a much more important and decisive element in government than the Parliament. Queen Elizabeth I had very wide and independent powers which she never hesitated to use. She was very much the sort of sovereign which Hobbes advocated. After the Civil War the representative part of government, the Parliament, grew in importance. Parliament not only made the laws, but it increasingly became necessary for the Crown to find as its principal officers and advisers people who had the support of the members of the House of Lords and the House of Commons. Once it became the practice of the Crown to appoint to the high offices of state only men who could command majority support in the Lords and Commons it can be said that Britain then had representative and responsible government.

In the long history of Parliament, from its first beginnings in the reign of Edward I, there was one matter central to the working of government which was connected with the origins and development of the representative element in English political life. This was taxation: the obligatory transfer of assets from the subject to the sovereign authority.

In the six centuries between the departure of the Roman legions and the collapse of Roman authority in Britain, until the Norman Conquest in 1066, kings in England had been warriors and lawgivers, but they had very little absolute power in the sense that the armies they commanded were their own and the laws they made were rules and regulations which they themselves devised and proclaimed. The armies they led were formations, led by men much like themselves, who were in many ways little kings in the places from whence they came: leaders of bands of farmers, foresters and workmen who took arms to defend themselves or to attack others. The laws the kings promulgated were very much the customs which the people already followed. The lawmaking of the kings did little more than clarify and make more certain the customs of the people, and the king's justice consisted in helping the already existing enforcement agencies to work more effectively by supervision and judgement from above and independent of parties in conflict. Kings had few financial resources, and were expected to carry out their public functions from the resources they themselves controlled in the shape of land and those who worked for them as servants, serfs and slaves. When kings went to war or progressed through their kingdom doing justice, they expected, but did not always receive, assistance, and the assistance given was in the form of services and goods such as food, cattle and gifts.

When William, Duke of Normandy, overthrew the last Anglo-Saxon king of England, and gained control of the country, he took into his own control much unused or under-used land, particularly large areas of forest. He dispossessed some of the defeated supporters of King Harold and distributed landed property, and the people who worked on the land, to his supporters. He further undertook an administrative task which was extraordinary in the eleventh century; he took an inventory

Westminster Hall, inside the Houses of Parliament, was the chief law court of England from 1224 until 1882. It was the scene of many famous trials, including those of Sir Thomas More (1535) and Charles I (1649), when this drawing was made

of his new realm: the Domesday Book. But William, the Conqueror, changed comparatively little. He was a great king because he conquered and greatly increased the economic resources which he controlled, but he did not alter fundamentally the fact that the king 'lived of his own', and did not possess any means of systematically and continuously transferring resources from his subjects to his government.

One of the fundamental issues of English political life, from the death of William the Conqueror in 1087 to the restoration of Charles II in 1660, concerned the financial resources of the Crown and whether or not the king and his officials had the power and authority to take from the subjects of the government what the Crown needed or wanted in the way of assets. This issue manifested itself in many forms and with a variety of outcomes. A great crisis came in the reign of King John (1199–1216), whose popular nicknames, Lackland and Softsword, epitomised his problems.

His failure to keep control of territory in France claimed by the English Crown diminished his resources. He tried to make good these losses by attacking the two richest and most influential interests in England: the Church and then the landed (and armed) nobility. The Pope placed England under an Interdict which can best be described as a summons to the English to embark upon a religious General Strike. The nobility dragged their feet in assisting John in his wars with the French king. This led to further losses of the Crown's power across the Channel, and at the battle of Bouvines in 1214 John and his allies were thrashed by the French.

There was nothing left for John to do except meet the representatives of the Church and the nobility at Runnymede. The nobles and churchmen who confronted John did not attempt to overthrow him or to dismantle the royal government. They demanded and they obtained from him a Great Charter, the Magna Carta. This was a contract 'for the betterment of our realm, by the council of our venerable fathers [here follows the names of eleven archbishops, bishops and abbots] and of our nobles [here follows the names of sixteen nobles] and of our other faithful men [who are nameless]'. The contract had sixty-three clauses, most of which were undertakings by the king not to abuse feudal contracts between the Crown and the Church, the nobility and the people by way of arbitrary exactions, seizures of property and abuses of feudal rights. The twelfth article is the germ of the principle: 'No taxation without representation.' It reads:

> Scutage or aid shall be levied in our kingdom only by the common counsel, except for the ransoming of our body [his brother Richard I had been

kidnapped on his way home from a Crusade], the knighting of our eldest son, and for once marrying our eldest daughter; and for these only a reasonable aid shall be taken. The same permission shall hold with regard to the aids of the city of London.

The wealthiest interests in medieval England were the Church and the nobility, who drew their revenues from landed property and the tenants, serfs, servants, monks and nuns who worked these properties. But there were other sources of wealth: the free farmers who owned land not under the control of either the Church or the landed magnates and the craftsmen and merchants of the towns and cities.

In the century which followed the Great Charter of 1215 there was so much change and development in English society that the kind of government operated by John and by his successor, Henry III, became increasingly feeble and confused, and the community was afflicted by civil war. Edward I (1272–1307) brought some order out of conflict by creating a new type of great council which brought together not just the great churchmen and the great nobility but the lesser nobility; the knights of the shires and the burgesses of the towns. In the writ of summons, explaining what he intended, King Edward used the famous phrase, 'let that which toucheth all be approved by all'. Thus was Parliament brought into being—not the first body so called, but one which can rightly be described as the Model Parliament.

From the King's point of view, Parliament became a means of levying taxes on property and commerce, but the transfer of assets from subjects to government never became a one-way system. Taxes became a matter of bargaining. The King asked and explained why he needed money; the Parliament asked for action by the government in some area of concern to the Members of Parliament—both Lords and Commons. Edward I, for example, persecuted and robbed the Jews in order to replenish his Treasury, but when he expelled all of them in 1290, Parliament granted him a tax called a 'fifteenth', which he was still collecting sixteen years later. Thus the King was able to satisfy the fanaticism of his subjects, remove the competitors of the merchants and bankers, and make a profit for his government extracted from his grateful subjects. By this process of bargaining about taxes, the interests represented in Parliament were able to influence the policies of the government and the character of the laws made. The abiding feature of representative government is bargaining between representatives and the sovereign power, and among the representatives themselves.

There were many ups and downs in the long, slow development of parliamentary government in England, but this representative body was never absent or inoperative for long periods of time, as was the case on the continent of Europe, where bodies like Parliament survived only in the Netherlands, Switzerland and, in an attenuated, aristocratic form in Venice. Until after the English Civil War and the victory of the Parliamentary forces over the Crown, there can be no doubt that the Crown was much the strongest factor in the process of Government. When it ceased to be so, power did not pass to Parliament. Anarchy set in as it did during the Wars of the Roses. The final victor in the Wars of the Roses, Henry Tudor, established a strong, royal authority with many of the characteristics of the absolute sovereign which Hobbes advocated, but neither Henry VII nor his successors dispensed with Parliament, nor was the right to vote or withhold taxes suspended or ended. The King was still expected to live 'of his own' except in circumstances such as war, which required extraordinary expenditure. Much of the domestic politics of Tudor times can be explained in terms of the kings or the queens attempting to 'live of their own' without seeking financial assistance from Parliament. Henry VII kept down his expenses by avoiding the most expensive of all the royal activities, foreign wars, and he ruthlessly, and with profit to himself, dealt with the nobility who were on the losing side in the Wars of the Roses. His son, Henry VIII, was extravagant both in his domestic expenditure on public magnificence and on largely unsuccessful wars and political intrigues on the Continent, but he was careful not to ask too much of Parliament. Instead, he nationalised part of the lands of the Church, and then sold them off to private investors. He debased the currency, and brought on inflation, which is a form of taxation unauthorised by anybody; beneficial to some and detrimental to many.

The Tudor age was one of very great changes, both in Britain and abroad. The Tudor sovereigns were very active in bringing about change at home and meeting the challenge of the Catholic powers on the Continent, particularly the greatest and richest of them all, Spain. In all of this, the Tudor kings and queens involved Parliament, with the result that the great statutes which organised and reorganised the Church, controlled labour relations, instituted a system of welfare for the poor and provided for the protection of the Crown and the state against treason and conspiracy organised abroad were initiated by the Crown but made legal and given political support by the representatives of the nobility, the Church, the freemen of the counties and the major interests in the towns. Representative government became an effective system, because many men learned how to work and to develop an institution which gave a numerous political élite, drawn from all parts of the country, a say in public affairs.

The members of the Lords and the Commons of England had

influence, but not power. This belonged to the Crown, and it was employed with great determination and ruthlessness. Elizabeth I, in particular, dealt roughly and firmly with her enemies at home and abroad, and she would not tolerate interference or even a too-extended comment on her policies. The rack was much in use, the public executioners had plenty of work and the Tower of London was a busy prison and not a tourist attraction. Elizabeth was a popular sovereign. In our day we talk about the 'Falklands factor', i.e. the popular admiration for the Prime Minister because she determinedly stood up to a violent challenge from a Latin-American military dictatorship. Elizabeth stood up to the greatest power in Europe which threatened the independence of England.

The majority of the English people identified themselves with their Queen in her defiance of her enemies. She herself was an active popular politician, and in the presence of criticism in the Parliament or elsewhere she never hesitated to speak out. But she was full of guile. When the House of Commons came to the conclusion that one of its number, Peter Wentworth, the member for Tregony in Cornwall, had gone too far in his arguments about the Queen's government, they ordered him to prison in the Tower, but Elizabeth let him out. On the other hand, she went herself to Parliament where the members fell on their knees when she spoke, and she ticked them off with great severity. However, neither Elizabeth nor the Parliament had any illusions about the nature of government. The English government was based on law, and the Queen governed in accordance with the law. In short, English government was constitutional, representative government, even though the sovereign had an extensive prerogative power; that is, the power to do as the King or Queen and their officers thought best in the circumstances, and to do so without question.

One thing the Crown could not do legally was to levy taxes without the consent of Parliament. Certain of the Crown's revenues came from the Crown's own property; some from traditional feudal dues payable by nobles and knights; some, like customs duties, were granted automatically by Parliament for the life of the sovereign; and some, like ship money, could be levied by the Crown to meet an emergency. Taxes on property and the incomes from property, however, could only be levied with the consent of Parliament, both in the matter of the amount and the period of time in which the tax was applicable. This, and the absence of a standing, professional army, were the keys to the future development of government in Britain. The Crown did not have a secure financial base for independence and absolute control, and it lacked the disciplined force necessary to compel the community to transfer assets to the government. Furthermore, the Crown was obliged to operate in the presence of, and rule over, a community of moderate size and number, a proportion of whom understood the nature of politics, law and government, and had a long-standing experience of them.

Such was the state of affairs when the House of Stuart came to the thrones of the joint realms of England and Scotland. James I was described at the wisest fool in Christendom, a man of considerable learning, a bad judge of character and a disposition to theorise about politics and government. He was succeeded on the throne by his son, Charles I, a man of elegant taste, a good husband and father, a devoted Christian and of indecisive political judgement. Whether the first two Stuarts were the cause of the breakdown of government which produced the Civil War is an open question. It is certainly the case that they lacked the political flair so evident in Elizabeth I, whose 'love tricks', to use the words of Sir John Harrington, enabled her to dominate and lead the Parliament and galvanise the enthusiasm of her people. Money became the central issue between the Stuart Kings and Parliament. As tempers flared, Parliament became increasingly determined to control or humiliate the King by limiting or refusing taxes. The King turned to find his revenues from sources outside the control of Parliament, or allegedly so. The most famous example was ship money, which originally could lawfully be levied on port towns to build ships for the Royal Navy. Charles I levied it on all towns, whether ports or not. He made the dreadful political mistake of seeking to increase his power by relying on the arms of his other kingdoms, first Scotland and then Ireland. The Parliament attacked his servants, and eventually passed an Act of Attainder against one of his great officers, the Earl of Stafford. This meant simply that by an Act of Parliament Stafford's head was cut off. Stafford pleaded with his master to assent to his attainder in order to secure the peace of the kingdom. This was far from being the result. Civil War followed: the majority of the Parliament on one side; the King, his officers and a minority of Parliament on the other.

When the Civil War started neither side possessed well-organised armies. Parliament and the main supporters of Parliament had the means of financing war and, in the persons of Oliver Cromwell and Lord Fairfax of Cameron, the will and the ability to build an efficient armed force. Fairfax was an experienced soldier who had fought in Europe. Cromwell was a squire and working farmer, as well as being a Member of Parliament, of whom little notice had been taken in the events leading up to the Civil War. He was a Puritan who showed some evidence of religious fanaticism, but, in many things, Cromwell, to use his own words, had the root of the matter in him. He saw the need for a well-disciplined army, whose soldiers were well paid, well trained and recruited without distinction of class or religion. 'Give me,' he said, 'such men as had the fear of God before them and as made some conscience of what they did . . . the plain russet-coated captain that knows what he fights for and loves what he knows.' Out of such men, Cromwell made the New Model Army, the real beginnings of the modern British Army.

This army conquered all, and at sea the Navy defeated the Dutch, who were opposed to the British Navigation Acts, which gave to British shipping a monopoly of transport to and from British ports at home and overseas. Cromwell may have been a Member of Parliament, but he would tolerate no control by Parliament. When he discovered members seeking to negotiate with the King, he sent Colonel Pride with a detachment of soldiers to purge from Parliament those who sought to negotiate. Those not purged were called 'the Rump'. This in its turn was expelled. Charles was executed. A nominated Parliament was called; then a wholly new Parliament based on a written constitution was assembled. Cromwell was not pleased with this assembly. He dismissed it, divided England into twelve military districts, each in the charge of a major-general. All this was financed by a 10 per cent levy on the royal estates and such other taxes as the Lord Protector, which was Cromwell's title, thought proper.

So long as Cromwell lived, this system of government endured, for Cromwell was an impressive man and a great soldier who conquered wherever he commanded in Scotland and Ireland as well as in England. When he died and was succeeded by his son, Richard, his system fell apart very quickly. The English people, and particularly the men of property in town and countryside, were too long experienced in politics and too used to influence in public affairs to tolerate a day longer than necessary a government staffed in the main by narrow-minded, bigoted Puritans with swords in their hands, cannon at their backs and cant on their lips.

The monarchy was restored and with it the Parliament as it existed before the Civil War. But much had changed. Charles II declared that he did not want to go on his travels again, and much of the legislation designed to limit the power of the Crown and to ensure the independence of Parliament was retained. All feudal exactions on which the Crown had depended as an independent source of revenue were abolished, and the King was given an assured annual grant for life of £1,200,000. Additional revenue required by the Government could only come from taxes and duties levied by Parliament. The size of the army was reduced from 30,000 to 5,000.

Charles II was a cautious, cynical and light-hearted man who never

Cromwell dismissing Parliament in April 1653, telling members that they 'have sate long enough'. The next day someone pinned a 'To Let' notice on the door of the House of Commons

made the mistakes of his father and grandfather. Unfortunately, his brother, James, who succeeded him on the throne inherited much of his grandfather's foolishness with the added handicap that he was a Roman Catholic fanatic who believed he could restore the Roman Catholic Church in Britain. To suppose that this was possible in England and Scotland amounted to madness, but James persisted. A number of influential people among the nobility, in the Church, in the army and in the City of London got together in opposition to the king, and explored the possibility of inviting his daughter, Mary, and her husband, the Prince of Orange, to take the throne. James departed and William and Mary arrived. Thus was the Glorious Revolution of 1688 accomplished.

The Convention Parliament which offered the throne to William and Mary as joint sovereigns accompanied the offer with a Declaration or Bill of Rights. This is the nearest thing there is to a general, legally binding British constitution. All the Bill did was reaffirm in a brief way what was already law. The only really new provision was that which took from the Crown the right of raising and keeping a standing army in time of peace. This power was henceforward based on a statute, passed by Parliament annually in the form of the Mutiny Act, which fixed the size of the military establishment and authorised the maintenance of military discipline.

Because many of the ideas and policies contained in the Bill of Rights of 1689 echo through the Constitution of the United States of America and reveal a great tradition in politics which, for all their differences, link together the American and British democracies, the reader ought to pause long enough to study and, if possible, memorise the following:

> And therefore the said lords spiritual and temporal and commons pursuant to their respective letters and elections being now assembled in a full and free representative of this nation, taking into their most serious consideration the best means for attaining [their] ends . . . do in the first place (as their ancestors in like case have usually done) for the vindicating and asserting of their ancient rights and liberties, declare that the pretended power of suspending of laws or the executing laws by regal authority without the consent of parliament is illegal; that the pretended power of dispensing with laws or the execution of laws by royal authority, as it hath been assumed and exercised of late, is illegal . . . that levying money for, or to the use of, the Crown by pretence of prerogative without grant of parliament, for longer time or other manner than the same is or shall be granted, is illegal; that it is the right of the subjects to petition the king, and all commitments [to prison] and prosecutions for such petitioning are illegal; that the raising or keeping a standing army within the kingdom in

time of peace, unless with the consent of parliament is against law; that subjects which are Protestants may have arms for their defence suitable to their conditions and as allowed by law; that the election of members of parliament ought to be free; that the freedom of speech and debates or proceedings in parliament ought not to be impeached or questioned in any court or place out of parliament; that excessive bail ought not to be required, nor excessive fines imposed, nor cruel and unusual punishments inflicted; that jurors ought to be duly impanelled and returned, and jurors which pass upon men in trials for high treason ought to be freeholders; that all grants and promises of fines and forfeitures of particular persons before conviction are illegal and void; and that redress for all grievances and for the amending and strengthening and preserving of the laws, parliaments ought to be held frequently . . .

The purpose of this Bill of Rights was to oblige the Crown and its officers in the Government to carry on its activities in accordance with the law as it existed; to do nothing independently of Parliament; not to make use of its powers to intimidate individuals or to make bargains with them under threats; and not to equip itself with an armed force unless authorised by Parliament. The Bill of Rights did not limit the activities of government; it did nothing more than require the operation of government to be conducted in accordance with the law, in the making of which Parliament would have a share. The government could in principle, declare black to be white or likewise convert all private property into communal property and such would be legal, provided Parliament approved.

In the years following the Glorious Revolution of 1688, England and then Britain (for Scotland united itself with England in 1707) enjoyed an astonishing success in terms of ecomomic development, expansion overseas and military victories on the continent of Europe and elsewhere. England and Scotland ceased to be small powers on the edge of Europe. As Britain, they moved to the centre of the world political stage, clouding the glory of the Sun King of France, Louis XIV, and blotting out that of his successor, Louis XV.

This success provoked foreigners and Englishmen themselves to ask the question, 'Why?' A French intellectual and aristocrat, Montesquieu, lived for some time in Britain between 1728 and 1731. He came to the conclusion that the secret of British success was liberty, something which did not exist under the absolute monarchies of continental Europe. This was very much in line with the British explanation, stated in serious writing on politics by men like the Marquis of Halifax and John Locke, and in popular boasts about 'free-born' Englishmen and the British Constitution.

Montesquieu's analysis did not attribute the liberty which he believed to characterise Britain to the innate virtues of the British people, or to a superior system of morals, but to the structure of the British system of government. Montesquieu did not fully understand the British constitution, and much of his analysis was, if not entirely wrong, not completely right either. But he was right in noting that government in Britain did differ significantly from the absolute monarchies of continental Europe in as much as the tasks of governments were split between the Crown and its officers, the representative Parliament and the judges who determined particular applications of the law in civil and criminal matters. The British were a free people because some, at least, participated in the making of the laws; the Crown and its officers were bound by the law and the application of the law was in the hands of judicial officers independent of the Crown and the Parliament. There was in Britain a separation of powers, as there was supposed to have been in the Roman Republic.

This doctrine of the separation of powers had an enormous influence upon future constitution-making, and particularly among the Americans after their separation from Britain. A key word in the doctrine was 'balance'. It was not denied that government was a sovereign authority in the community, but it was asserted that the activity of governing had three aspects or departments, as it were. There was the executive power, which kept order in the community, protected it from enemies and made arrangements with friendly foreign governments. In Britain the executive was the Crown and the officers and agencies of the Crown, such as the armed forces on land and at sea. This was the oldest part of the government, for the kings of England had always been leaders in war, lawgivers and judges. Then there was Parliament, the lawmaking body. This dated from the thirteenth century, and had gradually developed the legislative function after the Civil War and the restoration of the monarchy in 1660. The business of lawmaking became the predominant activity of Parliament, although laws then, as they formally still do, required the assent of the sovereign. The Crown might propose legislation but legislation required the majority assent of both Houses of Parliament. It is fair to say that the Parliament after 1660 was the lawmaking branch of government. Then there were the judges or, to use a general term, the judiciary. Judges, in the beginning, were the servants of the sovereign and long remained so. In the reign of James I and Charles I one famous judge, Sir Edward Coke, asserted his independence of the Crown, but it was not until the Act of Settlement passed by Parliament in 1701 that the commission of appointment of judges entitled them to hold office and receive fixed salaries so long as they behaved themselves, and they could only be removed by an address to the Crown passed by both Houses of

Parliament. Thus, the judges became, in practice, independent of the Crown and subject only to removal for bad behaviour proven to the satisfaction of a majority in Parliament.

It was believed that this tripartite form of government, made up of the executive, the legislature and the judiciary, produced a balance so that no one agency of government had independent power. Each, it was argued, checked the other. Parliament itself was divided into a House of Lords and a House of Commons which balanced each other, and in the House of Commons the representatives of the boroughs balanced the representatives of the counties. From this complicated balancing-act there emerged the great prize of liberty enjoyed by free-born Englishmen, Scotsmen and Irishmen.

Such was the theory, and there was something in it, but not everything. The liberty which the British esteemed in their political institutions became a central enthusiasm among the men and women who made the American Revolution and the Constitution of the United States of America. Liberty became for them a prime objective. The preamble of their constitution is brief. It reads:

> We, the People of the United States, in order to form a more perfect Union, establish Justice, ensure domestic Tranquility, provide for the common Defence, promote the general Welfare, and secure the Blessings of Liberty to ourselves and our posterity, do ordain and establish this Constitution for the United States of America.

How did they go about this? What structure of government did they establish? Upon what theory did they build?

We have already called brief attention to some facts of modern society which make the idea of democracy and equality seem natural and inevitable. Migration of Europeans to North America, which began early in the seventeenth century, and steadily increased, produced the same change and social flexibility which, in Europe, has been associated with industrial development. The migration of Europeans to a vast and bountiful continent only thinly populated by primitive Indians, who were hard to catch and difficult to enslave (and who as traders in furs readily and rapidly adapted themselves to the commercial life of the newcomers), was a transforming factor stronger than any ideas the newcomers may have had about the right and proper ordering of society. Life in the colonies, in North America, British, French and Dutch, soon lost some of the hierarchical character it had in Europe. The most important factor in this was the abundance of land and resources, the scarcity of people to engage in productive work and the always present opportunity for those who did not want to work for others either to move on and set up on their own, or simply to drop out and 'go native'. The easy rider, who mounts his motor bike and, leaving all behind him, tries to scratch a living by casual work or theft, has a spiritual ancestor in America in the man who, with a gun in his hands, and a pack on his back—and even without a gun—used, like Huckleberry Finn, to 'light out for the territories' or turn *courier du bois* in the French possessions.

In these circumstances which prevailed in British North America in the seventeenth and eighteenth centuries, the ideas of liberty, freedom and equality began naturally to prevail. And so did their opposite: chattel slavery. The difficulties of recruiting labour except on terms reasonably agreeable to the labourers was the most important factor in the enslavement of blacks, who could be purchased in large numbers on the west coast of Africa.

In the British–American colonies liberty and slavery developed side by side. Contemplating the question of what is the best form of government, the Americans, like the ancient Greeks, assumed that women and slaves did not count. Everyone else did.

Or nearly everyone else. In Britain voters in the elections of the Members of the House of Commons were, in general, property owners. In the English counties there was a uniform franchise, or right to vote; it belonged to the 'forty-shilling freeholders'. That meant in possession of land worth forty shillings a year or more. In the towns the franchise varied enormously, from the 'rotten' boroughs, where the landowners, who were often very few in number, returned two Members of Parliament, to some unusual boroughs like Westminster, where all resident males voted. In the British North American colonies the same relationship between the property and participation in political life prevailed. The men who voted, and those who sat in the colonial legislatures, were men of property. But there was a difference in the colonies. More men possessed property in America than in Britain. Furthermore, no colonial equivalent of Parliament had a separate house filled with hereditary nobles who were not elected but sat as of right, and were not just property-owners, but great landed proprietors.

An important factor in the coming, and then the triumph, of the American Revolution was the existence in the colonies of British North America of a numerous class of people—probably larger in proportion to that of Britain—who had active experience of politics as voters and members of colonial legislative assemblies. They understood the issues of politics in much the same way as did the British, and recognised very well that the key to the influence and control of government was the matter of taxation, and that the separation of powers was something one took seriously. In an important sense the British North Americans were very British in their politics—even more so, it may be argued. That is why they did away with monarchy, not temporarily as Cromwell did in England, but permanently, and created in North America a republic.

The United States of America is the largest democratic republic in the world and, save the Swiss Republic, the oldest. No student of politics anywhere can fully understand the working of democratic government and its problems who does not study the United States—its theoretical foundation, its structure, its working and its political practices.

The United States of America was not at the time of establishment a democracy, but by working the institutions established by the Constitution, presented to the world on 17 September 1787, it has become one, a state whose chief executive officer, the President, is elected every four years by a body of voters comprised of every man and woman in the United States, being citizens, regardless of colour, economic condition or political affiliation or religious faith. And not only its chief executive is elected, but every man and woman who serves in its lawmaking bodies and, in some cases, its judges. Views may differ about the policies and the place of the United States in the world, but whatever the United States may seem to others, it is a democracy, and can only be understood and judged as such. And democracy, too, can be judged by its exemplar, the United States of America.

The men who gathered in Philadelphia in May 1787 to consider the articles of confederation under the terms of which the revolutionary colonies had governed themselves and achieved their independence were, on the whole, young in years—Alexander Hamilton was only thirty and James Madison thirty-six—but old in political experience and the heirs of a tradition reaching back for 500 years. Indeed, they grasped and seriously understood the political thinking of the ancient Greeks and the Roman Republic and Empire. However, they were not imitators. They had their own ideas and a rich fund of experience which they brought to the extraordinarily difficult task facing them.

Three of the participants in the convention, Alexander Hamilton, James Madison and John Jay, published a number of articles in the newspapers over the pseudonym *Publius*, which enable us to learn something of the ideas of the men who made the Constitution. These they brought together and published in a volume of essays; *The Federalist*.

They were quite clear on one essential point: 'The vigour of government is essential to the security of liberty,' and 'nothing is more certain than the indispensable necessity of government . . .'

They accepted what had become a fashionable view among

eighteenth-century political thinkers from John Locke onward, that men and women have self-evident natural rights such as those stated in the American Declaration of Independence: life, liberty and the pursuit of happiness. It is necessary to add, however, that Locke was no sentimentalist and he did not say anything about happiness which cannot be pursued in itself, but is always the by-product of something else. Locke said 'Property and Estate'.

If the makers of the Constitution of the United States had merely argued on behalf of natural rights, their thoughts would have soon been forgotten, and it is unlikely that their Constitution would have amounted to anything durable. Natural rights were taken for granted. The problem was to secure them and make them operational in real life. So they turned to consider what men and women, and society, are really like; what men and women, for all that they are endowed with natural rights, actually do and do to one another.

Any well-constructed state must 'break and control the violence of faction'. A faction is 'a number of citizens, whether amounting to a majority or a minority of the whole, who are united and actuated by some common impulse of passion, or of interest, adverse to the rights of other citizens, or to the permanent and aggregate interests of the community'.

Liberty is to faction what air is to fire. If you have liberty you have faction. 'There are two methods of removing faction: the one is to destroy liberty which is essential to its existence; the other, by giving every citizen the same opinions; the same passions and the same interests.' This is the Fascist and Communist solution of the problem. Madison anticipated the possibility of a Lenin or a Hitler. He was at least a century before his time. His only mistake was in supposing that these methods for suppressing faction can be used separately. They are always used together.

Because Madison's analysis of the natural antagonisms in modern society is more profound and more comprehensive than anything in Marx and Engels, or in the writings of anarchists like Bakunin and Kropotkin, it is worthwhile quoting from the tenth essay in *The Federalist*:

> As long as the reason of man continues fallible, and he is at liberty to exercise it, different opinions will be formed. As long as the connnection subsists between his reason and his self-love, his opinions and his passions will have a reciprocal influence on each other; and the former will be objects to which the latter will attach themselves. The diversity in the faculties of men, from which the rights of property originate, is not less an insuperable obstacle to a uniformity of interests. The protection of these faculties is the

first object of government. From the protection of different and unequal faculties of acquiring property, the possession of different degrees and kinds of property immediately results; and from the influence of these on the sentiments and views of the respective proprietors, ensues a division of the society into different interests, and parties.

The latent causes of faction are thus sown in the nature of man; and we see them everywhere brought into different degrees of activity, according to the different circumstances of civil society. A zeal for different opinions concerning religion, concerning government, and many other points, as well of speculation as of practice; an attachment to different leaders ambitiously contending for pre-eminence and power; or to persons of other descriptions whose fortunes have been interesting to the human passions, have, in turn divided mankind into parties, inflamed them with mutual animosity, and rendered them much more disposed to vex and oppress each other than to co-operate for their common good. So strong is this propensity of mankind to fall into mutual animosities, that where no substantial occasion presents itself, the most frivolous and fanciful distinctions have been sufficient to kindle their unfriendly passions and excite their most violent conflicts. The most common and durable source of factions, however, has been the various and unequal distribution of property. Those who hold and those who are without property have ever formed distinct interests in society. Those who are creditors, and those who are debtors, fall under a like discrimination. A landed interest, a manufacturing interest, a mercantile interest, a moneyed interest, with many lesser interests, grow up of necessity in civilised nations, and divide them into different classes, actuated by different sentiments and views. The regulation of these various and interfering interests forms the principal task of modern legislation, and involves the spirit of party and faction in the necessary and ordinary operations of the government.

Thus the men who made the American Constitution accepted the fact that faction exists and its management, not elimination, is the business of government. Unlike philosophers and teachers such as Plato, and statesmen such as Philip II of Spain, Robespierre, the sea-green incorruptible French revolutionary leader, or Lenin, or Hitler or Stalin, or Mao Tse-tung, or Fidel Castro, Madison believed that liberty and the consequences of liberty are both necessary and desirable.

The inevitable 'propensity to faction' is the reason why no man can be allowed to be a judge in his own case; nor a legislator in his own interest nor an enforcer of the laws which benefit himself. Implicit in Madison's prescription is something more than the separation of powers, which European thinkers believed to be the key to liberty. The authors of the Constitution of the United States, of course, made the separation of powers a central feature of American government, but they expanded the idea. For them the legislative branch of government was the arena in which faction must flourish, where it must be brought into the open, and where contending interests and opinions must balance one another and, through the adjustments among them, the highest common factor in politics be discovered. The more factions there are, the less the likelihood of anyone of them overpowering the rest.

The authors of the Constitution copied the 'separation of powers' ground-plan of government which had been developed in Britain. Congress, not Parliament, was the name given to the legislative branch; the President replaced the monarch as the Executive Officer and as the sovereign in the international community; the Supreme Court was the judiciary. There was a further separation of powers completely unknown to the British system of government: the separation between the Government of the United States and the governments of several states which were the old British colonies. The state governments continued as before the Constitution of the United States was adopted, but the adoption of the Constitution meant the acceptance of the 10th Section of Article I, which required that 'no state shall enter into any treaty, alliance or confederation; . . . coin money; emit bills of credit; make anything but gold or silver coin a tender in payment of debt; pass any bill of attainder or *ex post facto* law; lay any levy or duties on exports . . . No state shall, without the consent of Congress, lay any duties of tonnage, keep troops or ships of war in time of peace, enter into any agreement or compact with another state, or with a foreign power, or engage in war unless actually invaded, or in such iminent danger as will not admit of delay.' What this amounted to was that the states ceased to be sovereign authorities in the international community, ceased to have any armed forces of their own and surrendered to the Federal Government their power over the money system and the flow of commerce across state boundary lines. One of the most important consequences of this was that the United States became at once the largest competitive free-trading area in the world, which it has remained from that day till this.

When the Constitution was first inaugurated the directly elected element in the government was limited to the House of Representatives; the lower House of Congress. The Senate, which was the equivalent of the House of Lords in the British Parliament, was not elected by the people. On the other hand, it was not an hereditary body of landed proprietors, bishops and law lords. It was a body representative of the states of the Union: two for each state regardless of size. Little Delaware and New Jersey each had two senators, the same as New York and Virginia. The Senators were appointed by the State legislature for six years. After the Civil War (1861–3) the demand developed for the direct election of Senators by the people. Some states in the Middle and Far West commenced the practice of popular voting which the State legislature accepted as mandatory in their election of senators. In 1912 the Seventh Amendment of the Constitution provided for the direct election of Senators in all states. Senators sit for six years, and one third of the Senate retire every two years, so that the total membership of the Senate is never up for re-election at the same time.

The President was similarly not elected by the people. In the Constitution, as originally adopted, the President and Vice-President were elected, like the Pope, by an electoral college. This was made up of persons appointed to the electoral college by the State legislatures by any method considered desirable. Each state appointed to the college a number of members equal to their representation in Congress, which meant two (being the number of their senators) plus the number of their representatives in the House of Representatives, which was determined by the population of the state. The first President, General George Washington, was elected by the electoral college prescribed by the Constitution, but thereafter different methods of choosing electors developed, so that, well before the Civil War, popular participation in the selection of the President and Vice-President was an established fact. The electoral college system still prevails, but the members of the electoral college are bound to vote for the candidates who have the most votes in the state. There are no restrictions on who runs for the Presidency, except that he or she must be a natural-born citizen of the United States, be thirty years old (at least) and a resident of the United States for at least fourteen years. Two prominent public figures of the 1960s and 1970s, John K. Galbraith, born in Canada, and Henry Kissinger, born in Germany, could not think of running for the Presidency, in spite of some support for them so doing.

The Supreme Court required by the Constitution is one branch of the government which has never been 'popularised' and open to the direct influence of the voters. The Constitution did not prescribe the membership of the Supreme Court or the method of choosing the judges. This was left to Congress, but the same rules, ensuring the independence of the judiciary as was established in the Act of Settlement of the British Parliament, are constitutional requirements. Judges of the Supreme Court and lesser federal courts hold office during good behaviour, and their salaries are guaranteed and cannot be reduced.

The Supreme Court and its independence of the executive and legislative branches of government is regarded by the majority of Americans with something approaching reverence. When, in the 1930s, the Supreme Court found unconstitutional some of the legislation establishing President F. D. Roosevelt's New Deal, he turned nasty and vowed to increase the size of the Supreme Court in order to outnumber the Nine Old Men, as he called them. This reform of the Supreme Court required Congressional legislation. The Congress absolutely refused to implement the President's plan to reform the Supreme Court and, for this stand by the Congress, there was very widespread support from the public. Significant numbers of both political parties spoke out against interference with judicial independence. Although Roosevelt was elected four times President of the United States, and the only man to be so elected, he failed to undermine the independence of the judiciary ordained by the Constitution.

Although it is not a democratically elected body, and perhaps because it is not, the Supreme Court has played an important part in the development of public policy in the United States of America. After the Civil War and the abolition of slavery, popular democracy, particularly in the ex-slave states, legislated to 'keep the niggers in their place'. Legislation imposing literacy tests on voters, laws segregating the races in public places, such as on trains and buses, in schools and universities, were passed and the Supreme Court ruled that so long as facilities were equal, which they seldom were, they could be segregated, which they normally were. In 1956, however, the Supreme Court consented to hear new evidence on the question of 'separate but equal' provision of public education, and as a result ruled that separate provision is not equal provision and that access to public services must be open to all. This did not solve completely the problem of segregation, but it destroyed its legal foundation. The gates were open for the achievement of a free and equal society in the United States. It is no longer impossible for an American black to be President as it was, say, in 1950.

The Constitution of the United States defines broadly but exactly the subjects about which the Congress can legislate. This definition was necessary, because the States already had the power of legislation, subject only to the limitations under Article I, Section 10, already described. But there was another reason for definition. The men who made the Constitution wanted positive government, but they did not want too much of it. Liberty was as important to them as government. Section 8 of Article I contains a list of 18 topics on which Congress can legislate. Eight of them relate to the control of the national economy: the power to tax, to borrow money, to regulate commerce with foreign states and, among the states of the United States of America, to coin money and to regulate its value; to establish post offices and post roads; to secure the property rights of authors and inventors in their own work;

Signs behind a bar in Montana, USA. That on the left, proclaiming 'Life, liberty and justice for all' is at odds with that forbidding beer to Indians

and to ensure the uniformity of bankruptcy laws. The remaining subjects of Congressional legislation have to do with legislating to establish courts inferior to the Supreme Court, to provide the means of enforcing American obligations under international law; to raise armies, and organise and discipline them; to build defence works. The 18th provision is a general one: 'To make all laws which shall be necessary and proper for carrying into execution the foregoing powers, and all the other powers vested by this Constitution in the government of the United States or in any department or office thereof.'

If the Congress has power to legislate, it is also denied the power to legislate on certain topics. This makes an interesting list. The first prohibits legislation on the slave trade until 1808, 'and the duty on imported slaves shall not exceed ten dollars a head'. The next is one much concerned with the liberty of the citizen, if not a slave. In 1679 the British Parliament passed the Habeas Corpus Act, which prohibits officers of the government from holding anyone in prison for more than three days without a charge being made and a reason given for imprisonment, and further required that the cases of people charged be heard at the earliest opportunity or else released; and further that prisoners may not be sent out of England to Scotland, Ireland, Jersey, Guernsey or overseas. The Constitution incorporates this guarantee against arbitrary imprisonment by the simple provision that 'the privilege of the writ of *habeas corpus* shall not be suspended unless when, in cases of rebellion or invasion, the public safety may require it'.

Congress is likewise prohibited from passing a bill of attainder, such as the Act of Attainder under the terms of which the English Parliament sentenced the Earl of Stafford to death, nor can Congress pass an *ex post facto* law, i.e. one which, for example, imposes penalties for crimes which were not crimes at the time they were committed. Unfortunately, no means has been found for protecting people from abuse and harassment on account of right political judgements when the majority were wrong and were proven wrong by events. Abuse for 'premature anti-Facism' springs to mind in this connection.

There are, too, prohibitions on fiscal action by Congress. Congress may not, for example, impose taxes on exports from any state, nor create by regulation or tax advantages for the commerce or the ports of one state over those of another. Money cannot be drawn from the Public Treasury unless authorised by law; and a public statement of public receipts and expenditures must be made.

The makers of the Constitution sought to preserve the republican form of government and to prevent the government of the United States and all foreign governments from bribing American citizens with titles of nobility, presents, offices and emoluments. Because of the Eighth Article of Section 9 of Article I of the Constitution, the Government of the United States of America does not possess so large a means as the British Government of recruiting political support by conferring social prestige upon its supporters. About the best the President and Congress can do for its supporters and office-holders is to dole out ambassadorships and commisionerships, which confer temporary social prestige.

The prohibitions on Government action proposed by the authors of the Constitution were rather limited in number. Before the Constitution was ratified, ten further Amendments, now referred to as the Bill of Rights, had to be adopted. These amendments put some real legal obstacles in the way of arbitrary government and the development of despotism and collectivist tyranny.

The First Amendment is a real 'law of liberty'. It reads:

Congress shall make no law respecting an establishment of religion, or prohibiting the free exercise thereof; or abridging the freedom of speech, or of the press; or the right of the people peaceably to assemble, and to assemble, and to petition the government for the redress of grievances.

The Second Amendment seeks to prevent a monopoly of armed forces in the hands of the government. It reads:

A well regulated militia, being necessary to the security of a free state; the right of the people to keep and bear arms shall not be infringed.

The Fourth Amendment seeks to prevent the harassment of citizens by the government:

The right of the people to be secure in their persons, houses and papers, and effects against unreasonable searches and seizures, shall not be violated, and no warrant shall issue, but upon probable cause, supported by oath or affirmation, and particularly describing the place to be searched and the persons or things to be seized.

If it is possible to erect barriers against tyranny and arbitrary government and to protect the individual against the state, the Fifth Amendment is the means of doing so. It reads:

No person shall be held to answer for a capital or otherwise infamous crime, unless on a presentment or indictment of a grand jury, except in cases arising in the land or naval forces or in the militia, when on actual service in time of war or public danger; nor shall any person be subject for the same offence to be twice put in jeopardy of life or limb; nor shall be compelled in any criminal case to be a witness against himself, nor be deprived of life, liberty, or property, without due process of law; nor shall private property be taken for public use without compensation.

The Fifth Amendment ties the hands of government in many matters, and on that account it has been much criticised because it makes life easier for criminals and enemies of democratic government. It has been objected, too, that the Fifth Amendment spins out the legal process and makes work for lawyers. There is some substance to these criticisms and objections, but these are petty points when one considers that the final two dozen words of the Fifth Amendment make it legally impossible to establish a totalitarian regime—Fascist, Communist or militarist—in the United States.

Individuals and organised groups have suffered many injustices at the hands of governments in the long history of the United States of America, but the Fifth Amendment is part of the political conscience of the American people and a legal obstacle to the development of torture, concentration camps for dissidents and coercive bullying by people in power. We know from experience that governments can go to unimaginable lengths in the injustice practised on their victims. If this has not happened in the United States on the scale that it has in the Soviet Union, in China, in Cuba, in Iran and many other places, it is because the Constitution of the United States of America, as amended at the time of its ratification by the several states, has created a moral understanding and a legal structure of government which makes difficult the terrible excesses to which men and women are only too prone when they have power and are in the grip of illusions of omniscience.

We live in an age of 'big governments', whose strength may destroy us all. The Tenth Amendment of the Constitution, however, is a kind of hope. It reads:

The powers not delegated to the United States by the Constitution, nor prohibited by it to the States, are reserved to the States respectively, or to the people.

That it can be supposed that the ultimate power and what is not delivered to a government for specific purposes belongs to men and women in general is a hope for mankind, and worth thinking about.

There is another feature of the Constitution which must be considered. No officer of the United States' government is immune from prosecution for misbehaviour, the abuse of power or law-breaking. All are liable to impeachment for 'high crimes and misdemeanours'. Once a bill of impeachment is passed by Congress the person impeached is tried by the Senate. When a President of the United States is impeached, the Senate sits under the presidency of the Chief Justice, and conviction requires a two-thirds majority of the Senate. President· Andrew Johnson was impeached in 1868, and escaped conviction by only one vote. In 1974 President Richard Nixon resigned in order to avoid impeachment on the grounds that he had violated his oath of office 'to preserve, protect and defend the Constitution of the United States'. Although few have ever been impeached, the possibility of being so has prompted resignations. The important principle in fact is this: in the American systen no-one can escape responsibility for what they do as public servants in any branch of government. Of course many do, but doing so is a crime, not a privilege.

When the American people confirmed by treaty their independence of the mother-country in 1783, Britain was no more democratic than the newly born United States. It was, however, somewhat further along the road to democracy inasmuch as slavery, for example, had been pronounced illegal in Britain by Lord Chief Justice Mansfield in 1772, and slavery was ended everywhere in the British Empire in 1833, thirty years before the Americans did so. In general, however, the Americans and British marched at a similar pace along the same democratic path. In a series of reform acts beginning with the first reform bill of 1832, more and more people in Britain were given the right to vote in Parliamentary elections. By 1884 all men had the vote. In 1918 the vote was given to women over 30 years of age, subject to a property qualification. By 1928 every adult over 21 years had the right to vote, and in 1976 the age limit for voting was reduced to 'over 17'.

In 1911 the House of Lords was deprived of its right to veto legislation passed by the House of Commons. In 1956 the principle of hereditary membership (except in the case of law lords and archbishops and bishops) was breached by legislation empowering the government to appoint life peers. As a result, the House of Lords has become a very large body of approximately 1,200 members, the majority of whom seldom, or never, attend. Unlike the American Senate, the British House of Lords has no direct relationship with the electorate, nor has it any specific powers of its own. It can, and does, review the work of the House of Commons, but it can only delay legislation.

The Queen-in-Parliament is an absolute sovereign inasmuch as an Act of Parliament, which in fact is automatically signed by the monarch, is mandatory for all citizens, and can only, with extreme difficulty, be challenged in the courts. Until Britain entered the European Economic Community, British subjects had, in practice, no rights against Parliament and its legislation. Now it is possible for British sub-jects to appeal to the European Court on Human Rights against the legislation of Parliament, and some have done so successfully in the matter of compulsory membership in trade unions. There can be little doubt that Britain requires a modern bill of rights which protects the individual against the omnipotent power of Parliament. In this respect the British Constitution needs to become more like the American Con-stitution if democracy is to be surely preserved against its internal enemies and their external allies.

Representative and responsible government, of which the govern-ments of the United Kingdom and the United States are long-standing examples, is the normal pattern of democratic governments everywhere. Even in the pseudo-democracies where the governments never lose elections, and the personnel of government grow old in office, or where the succession has become hereditary, as it has in the People's Demo-cratic Republic of (North) Korea, constitution-making tends to follow the ground-plan of the Constitution of the United States insofar as the structure of government is concerned; the separation of powers into legislative, executive and judicial branches, bills of rights and guaran-tees of periodical elections. Reading the Constitution of the USSR, one might suppose that it is a copy of the federal structure of the United States, and that the rights which it guarantees to Soviet citizens are much more comprehensive than the American bill of rights. How wonderful to have a constitutional right to employment, welfare benefits and the benefits of 'planned socialist production'! Is not Article 127 of the Constitution of the USSR so much more definite than the few words in the Fifth Amendment of the Constitution of the United States? It reads: 'The citizens of the USSR are guaranteed inviolability of per-son. No person may be placed under arrest except by decision of court or with the sanction of a procurator.' Splendid! But how can one explain the sudden arrest of Alexander Solzhenitsyn because he wrote a few words of criticism of Stalin in a private letter to a friend? How can one explain that similar arrests for even less reason, or no reason at all, were the experience of millions of Soviet citizens? These questions are pro-voked not only by the testimony of the survivors, but by the extensive statements of the First Secretary of the Communist Party of the USSR and President of the Presidium of the Supreme Soviet of the USSR, N. Khrushchev.

The differences between the real democracies and the pseudo ones of the Fascist, Communist and militarist types cannot be discovered primarily in their constitutions, but mainly in their political processes and practices, and the ideologies from whence they derive.

The principal pseudo-democracies are today the Marxist totalitarian states. Their political processes and practices illustrate the differences between the democracies and their pseudonymous imitators.

In the real democracies there is competition among the factions and interests in the community for the control of the representative and executive branches of government. In the totalitarian democracies there is none. One party always has a monopoly in the Marxist democracies. Article 126 of the Constitution of the USSR ensures this monopoly. It reads:

> In conformity with the interests of the toilers, and in order to develop the organisational initiatives and political activity of the masses of the people, citizens of the USSR are ensured the right to unite in public organisations— trade unions, co-operative associations, youth organisations, sport and defence organisations, cultural, technical and scientific societies; and, the most active and politically-conscious citizens, in the ranks of the working class and other strata of the toilers unite in the Communist Party of the Soviet Union [Bolsheviks] which is the vanguard of the toilers in their struggle to strengthen and develop the socialist system and which represents the leading core of all organisations of the toilers, both public and state.

No political competition here. No chance to form a Labour Party, a Liberal Party, a Conservative Party, a Democratic Party or a Republican Party. No place for a Christian Democratic Party or Ayatollahs or gurus. No place, in fact, for a workers' party. Solidarity in Poland has discovered that; the intellectuals in Charter 77 have had a similar experience in Czechoslovakia.

In the real democracies there are always to be found two or more political parties. These parties are private, not public, organisations. There may be, of course, legislation governing the organisation and financing of political parties, but such legislation does not give a preference to one party over another, nor prescribe a leading role to any one political party. In the real democracies the government for the time being must be neutral in respect of political parties. Such neutrality is hard to achieve, and partisan fanatics are always at work trying to use the power of the state to ensure party victories. Experience, however, demonstrates that legislation, backed by public awareness, can prevent monopoly control by single parties, and preserve open access to the political process. Open access means the right to nominate candidates for public office and the right of citizens to vote for them secretly.

Equally important in the real democracies is the opportunity to abstain from political activity. Seldom in a real democracy do more than 80 per cent of the eligible voters vote. Non-participation is a valid political stance. Not so in a totalitarian democracy. Close to 100 per cent of the electorate vote because voting is a means used by governments of discovering who lacks enthusiasm for the regime. Millions turn out to listen to Fidel Castro speak for three or four hours. A curious way of spending one's time it would seem, but quite explicable when there exists the apparatus for enquiring why one stayed at home or went to the beach. One indicator of effective freedom is the right to forget to vote without any questions being asked or any action being taken.

The most important difference between real democracy and pseudo, totalitarian democracy is the absence of official ideologies in real democracies and their presence in the totalitarian democracies. In the Fascist totalitarian states, which were more numerous before World War II than they are today, their ideologies were based on race. The Aryans, according to the German Nazis, were a unique race of supermen destined to rule the world. They believed that the white race, particularly the Germanic peoples, had special capacities and moral qualities which had been demonstrated by historical experience and that they were assigned by history to use or destroy other races in order to realise a glorious destiny for mankind. Everyone was obliged to believe this nonsense. Because it flattered the Germans many Germans did believe it, but some, like Pastor Neimöller, an ex-submarine commander of the German Navy and a Protestant pastor, as well as several Roman Catholic bishops, refused to do so. The Nazi police, the Gestapo, soon rounded up everyone; Communists, socialists, liberals and dissidents, and put them in concentration camps. Those who were supposed not to be Aryans, and particularly the Jews and the gypsies, were not just put in concentration camps; they were systematically murdered in gas chambers and by machine-gunning at the rate of hundreds of thousands a month. The total killed in this way exceeded 5,000,000.

Membership of the German National Socialist Workers' Party was an important qualification for everyone in the service of the government. The Nazi Party won power by a vote in the democratically elected Reichstag, but once in power the Nazis smashed up and suppressed all rival parties and put their leaders and many of their supporters in concentration camps, so ensuring that their critics never won any elections, nor indeed were ever heard again in the German community and, if possible, anywhere.

Racially based ideologies have diminished since World War II, and the principal instance of this type of ideology is to be found only in the South African Republic. Religiously based ideologies, however, have begun to develop strongly in the modern world. The most fanatical expression of this tendency has emerged in Iran. There the modernising,

A crematorium in a Nazi concentration camp at Weimar, Germany, containing the bones of women prisoners and discovered by American troops at the end of World War II

authoritarian regime of the Shah (or Emperor) of Iran was overthrown by a democratic movement composed of republicans, liberals, socialists, Communists and Islamic nationalists. The Islamic nationalists, led by a religious man, the Ayatollah Khomeini, organised a militia made up of young Muslim militants. They ruthlessly assaulted not only the Shah, but all those who did not share their fanatical religious doctrines. A reign of terror developed in which thousands perished. Opposition to the government was wiped out, and the officers of the government were themselves terrorised into doing the will of the ideological leader, Ayatollah Khomeini.

The largest and most powerful totalitarian states today depend upon Marxism as an ideology. Both the Soviet Union and the People's Republic of China, although bitterly opposed to each other, have a Marxist ideology. The same is true of Yugoslavia, which is anti-Soviet.

Marxists depend upon an interpretation of history for their faith. History, they argue, reveals that the workers are destined to inherit the earth and to build an ideal and perfect civilisation called 'Communism'. Not everyone, and certainly few historians, believe that this is so. An abundance of historical facts suggest otherwise. In order to ensure the 'truth' of their interpretation of history, the Marxists, who hold power in the USSR, China, Cuba and elsewhere, are obliged to suppress other interpretations of history and, indeed, all arguments that history has many meanings or none at all. Any deviation from the interpretation of history ordained by the Communist Party leaders who hold power is evidence of enmity to the government and is, therefore, a criminal activity punishable by suppression, exile, imprisonment and even death. The logic of Marxism requires a monopoly of political power in the hands of the party which preaches Marxism, and it likewise requires that the party of Marxism monopolises the power of the state.

In the real democracies there is no orthodox interpretation of either history or religion. What one thinks or believes is a matter of private judgement. People are free to think they know the whole truth and to preach any doctrine they like, but the political processes in the real democracies ensure that they can only force their beliefs on other people if they win majority support for their views. This is extremely difficult to do.

Of course, it is argued that in the real democracies beliefs are not as important as interest and pressure groups, and that the winning of elections benefits the winners in terms of economic advantage, social prestige and opportunities for propagandising on behalf of one's beliefs. This is so, but the constitutional requirement in the real democracies of periodic elections, secret voting and freedom of writing, printing and broadcasting, ensures that the opposition of the losers in one election is never suppressed nor is the hope of turning defeat into victory. And this does happen. The Republican Party in the United States of America does not always win, nor do the Democrats. In Britain the Conservatives do not always win, nor does the Labour Party. At one time the Liberal Party was thought to be the natural party of government; but the same was thought of the Conservative Party, and Lord Wilson once argued that this was true of the Labour Party. In fact, in a real democracy there is no natural party of government, no matter what political partisans at some particular time may suppose.

The control of the men with guns is important in the working of government. In the British case the dissolution of Cromwell's military dictatorship, the reduction in the size of the British Army and its control by Parliament by the Mutiny Act were absolutely indispensable for the growth of representative and responsible government. In the American case the Constitution gives to the President the power of Commander-in-Chief of the armed forces, so that an elected official is the man who gives the ultimate and final order to the soldiers and sailors who have in their hands the means of coercion. Additionally, the senior officers and, theoretically but not practically, all officers are appointed only with the approval of the US Senate. Furthermore, the financial provision for the armed forces is made by Congress. In both Britain and the United States members of the armed forces, when not on active service in war or civil insurrection, are subject to the same laws as citizens and have no special privileges or exemptions from ordinary legal obligations.

The politicians in the pseudo-democracies have perceived the problem of the armed forces in much the same way as the politicians in the real democracies. In Nazi Germany the high officers of the armed forces thought they controlled Adolf Hitler and the Nazis—but they soon learned otherwise. When some of these officers thought Hitler was losing the war and should be overthrown by violence they were ruthlessly strung up with piano wire or sent to concentration camps. In the Soviet Union the Communist Party never allowed the armed forces to think of themselves as rulers. The ranks were infiltrated with political commissars who watched in detail the activities of the officers at all levels in order to ensure the monopoly of power in the hands of the Communist Party. In the Soviet Union the armed forces are indoctrinated with Communist ideology as part of their military training, and it is seldom that a man rises to a high rank in the Soviet armed forces who is not a member—and a loyal member—of the Communist Party. Furthermore, a trained political police watches what goes on, and no matter what disguises a dissident may assume, he had little chance to seize power from the Party.

In other pseudo-democracies, particularly in the newer states of Africa and Asia, and in the older states of Latin America, the armed forces have managed to develop an independence of the politicians so that they hold power directly, as General Stroessner has done for thirty years in Paraguay, or they constitute a censorship group which dismisses politicians whom they do not like. For many years Argentina provided a prime example of this style of military control. There the armed forces were a self-selected group with guns in their hands. They believed that they were the ultimate custodians of the nation's interests and that this entitled them to overthrow governments and, when it seemed appropriate, to rule directly by selecting the civilian officers of the government, by overseeing their work and by determining the policies they were ordered to pursue. These were usually wrong and sometimes disastrously so.

There is another aspect of government which needs to be considered, and one which is very evident in all forms of government, democratic and pseudo-democratic alike. This is the growth and power of bureaucracy.

All governments require servants to carry out the policies they devise, and to administer the daily and continuous business of government: collecting revenue, applying the law, organising the services provided by the government to the citizens, and maintaining the peace and order without which nothing else is possible. The more a government undertakes to do, the more civil servants they require. When, of course, the politicians in power come to believe that the government must own and control everything, provide all the services the people need, or think they need, and regard themselves as possessed of a knowledge of what is best for the individual from the cradle to the grave and, what is worse, when people themselves believe they need have no free choice except about where to go for their holidays, then the demand for civil servants becomes enormous. The civil service then becomes a very big political interest on its own. The pay, promotion, pensions and privileges of the civil servant become of uppermost importance politically, for in the real democracies they become a very large voting interest and, in the pseudo-democracies the effective sources of all information available to the politicians of the monopoly party. The civil servants are there to serve but become masters. In the fifth century AD the Salian Franks invaded the Roman provinces of Gaul, and their leader Chlodis established himself as what may be called the first King of France. His sons and their grandson, Dagobert, established a sovereign authority, and to do this they needed servants. For more than two centuries the Merovingian monarchs ruled part of what is now Belgium and France. In the end, leading servants of the Merovingian kings, remembered as the Mayors of the Palace, took over the power of their masters, known as *les rois fainéants*, the royal loafers. What happened in Merovingian France 1300 years ago has happened frequently since, and is a very modern phenomenon. Dictators, Parliaments, Congresses and Presidents rule, but the effective power of making decisions and the profits of so doing can become the possession of the bureaucrats who pretend to know all and do all. Look around you and discuss.

5 Politics is about International Relations

It has already been stated that the world today is divided into 175 nation-states. These nation-states constitute the international community. This is not a community made up of individual men and women. Only in a metaphysical sense can one be a member of the human race. In practical terms every human being is a citizen of a nation-state, and is subject to the laws, rules and regulations of his or her nation. Generally speaking, one must be a citizen of one nation and only one nation. There are, however, nations whose governments allow dual citizenship, but even in the few instances where dual citizenship is permitted, the individuals enjoying this privilege are bound by the laws of the nation where they reside and cannot play off one government against another in the matter of obeying the law. As a general rule, one can assume that all individuals are citizens of one nation-state and of none other. If one is a member of one team, one cannot be a member of another team, and transfers, as any would-be immigrant knows, are sometimes difficult or impossible. Some states do not allow their citizens to leave; others do not allow the citizens of other states to settle in their territory and become citizens. Even when emigration and immigration are permitted, freely leaving and entering are subject to laws, rules and regulations, and it is no longer the case, as it was before World War I, that people move freely about the world settling, establishing themselves and becoming or not becoming citizens, according to their own wishes.

Theoretically, and to a considerable degree in practice, each nation-state is independent of the other nation-states in the international community. Each government does what it likes or what other nation-states allow it to get away with. It is a general rule, for example, that the jurisdiction of a state is exclusive and absolute in its own territory. This was certainly the case before World War I, when there were far fewer sovereign authorities in the world and large parts of it were under the sovereign authority of empires such as those of the British, French, Russian, Dutch, Portuguese, German, Austro-Hungarian, Italian and

Japanese. Today this sovereign independence of states is less clear.

Before World War I the sovereign authorities of that time were subject to international law. This law differed in important ways from the laws which prevailed in the sovereign states. First, the subjects of the law of the sovereign states were individuals or corporations (i.e. legally defined groups of citizens). International law, on the other hand, applied to the sovereign authorities themselves, and not to individuals or groups of individuals.

Second, international law was not made by any sovereign authority, because in the international community there was no sovereign. International law was made up of customs, of rules which sovereigns had agreed among themselves by treaties, of opinions about the rights and duties of sovereign states expressed by great international lawyers of the past, of precedents set by the past action of sovereign states, of the decisions made by arbitration in past disputes. The fundamental fact remained, however, that how much or how little of international law was accepted by a sovereign state depended upon the will of the sovereign state itself.

Many rules regarded as part of international law were of such utility to all concerned that no state challenged them. It was, for example, acknowledged by all for many years before World War I that the national territory of maritime states extended for three miles beyond the shore, and that national laws were operative at sea for this three miles, but not beyond. Great rivers which flowed through the territory of different nations, for example, the Rhine or the Danube, were regarded as international waterways on which ships of all nations could freely navigate. Before World War I people, too, freely travelled across state boundaries. The only European state which required travellers to show passports was Russia, but such was international law that there was no challenge to the right of the Russian Government to do this.

The third way in which international law differed from the laws of nation-states was the acceptance of the legality of violence as a means of settling disputes or differences. War was legal. There was, in fact, a large body of rules governing the waging of war, and some of them, such as the right to search on the high seas, were themselves the subject of disputes leading to war, for example, that between Britain and the United States from 1812 to 1814. Some of the rules of war were derived from the orders of chivalry of medieval times; some were the product of agreement among the sovereign states. The Red Cross organisation was established in the mid-nineteenth century to 'humanise' war by establishing rules governing the treatment of wounded soldiers, prisoners-of-war and civilians.

Nor were other forms of violence prohibited under international law.

In 1902 the Venezuelan Government refused to apply the law empowering foreigners in Venezuela to collect debts owing them by Venezuelan citizens. The response of the British, German and Italian Governments was to send a joint naval force to blockade the ports of Venezuela. The United States' Government then persuaded the parties in dispute to refer the trouble to arbitration. When the Venezuelans began to treat American citizens in Venezuela in the same way as they had treated the Europeans, the United States broke off diplomatic relations with Venezuela. When the Dutch were similarly treated, the Dutch navy blockaded Venezuelan ports. All this was quite in accordance with international law as it then existed, and the problem was only solved after the vice-president of Venezuela seized power while the president was in Europe for medical treatment.

The outbreak of World War I illustrates the way in which the 'old international law' worked, or did not work. First, the characters in the drama: the sovereign states involved. To begin with, there were only two states on the stage of history: the Austro-Hungarian Empire ruled by a very old royal family, the Hapsburgs, and Serbia, a comparatively new state of modest size which had gained its independence from the Turkish Empire. These two states were anything but friendly with each other. In 1908 the Austro-Hungarian Government had annexed two areas, Bosnia and Herzegovina, i.e. they had incorporated them into their territory and governed them and their people in the same way as the Hapsburg monarch governed his other territories such as Austria, Hungary, Bohemia and Slovakia. The Serbian Government did not like the incorporation of Bosnia and Herzegovina, but there was little the Serbs could do about it because the Austro-Hungarian Empire had a large and powerful army and many more resources of manpower and manufacturing capacity.

Late in June 1914 the Archduke Franz Ferdinand, the heir to the Austro-Hungarian throne, visited Bosnia and Herzegovina. On 28 June he was assassinated by a Bosnian revolutionary, Gavrilo Princip. So far, so bad. This was a crime committed by a subject of the Austro-Hungarian empire in the territory of that empire. No problem under international law.

The international legal position was simple enough, but not the political one. The assassin was a member of a revolutionary organisation, the Black Hand, which, though Bosnian in origin, was Slavic in membership and closely connected with similar organisations of Slavic nationalists in Serbia. The Austro-Hungarian government sought not only to punish the assassin but to root out the organisation of which he was a member. To do so was no offence against international law. But the Austro-Hungarian government went further. It did not ask the Serbian Government to take action against Bosnian revolutionaries in Serbia. This would have been a reasonable request, and one in conformity with long-recognised principles of international law that a state recognised as Serbia was by Austro-Hungary was bound not to engage in acts or permit its citizens to engage in unfriendly acts against another state. Instead, the Austro-Hungarian Government sent an ultimatum demanding that within 48 hours the Serbian Government suppress all propaganda against Austro-Hungary originating in Serbia, dissolve all anti-Austrian organisations in Serbia, remove all anti-Austrian material taught in state schools in Serbia, collaborate with Austro-Hungarian officials in hunting down those responsible for the assassination of the Archduke and to arrest two named Serbian officials allegedly involved in the assassination plot. If Serbia accepted these demands, Serbia would cease to be an independent sovereign state.

The Austro-Hungarian ultimatum to Serbia was extreme, but it was not contrary to international law. What it meant was that the laws of peace had been exhausted, and the laws of war were about to be invoked. To avoid this, the British Foreign Secretary, Sir Edward Grey, suggested an international conference to deal with the dispute and find a peaceful solution. The French and Russian governments supported this proposal, but the Austro-Hungarian Government refused. The Emperor of Austria-Hungary declared war on Serbia.

None of this was contrary to international law as it then existed, nor was anything which followed. Russia was allied by treaty with Serbia and was bound to come to Serbia's assistance if threatened. France was allied with Russia. Britain had no formal treaty arrangements with France and Russia, but the British Foreign Secretary had promised France and Russia assistance if they were attacked by Germany. Germany was allied to Austro-Hungary, and was bound to come to the assistance of Austro-Hungary if it were attacked by Russia. Britain had one treaty obligation: to come to the assistance of Belgium, if either Germany or France invaded Belgium. The British Government asked for a German undertaking not to enter Belgium. This was refused and when German troops crossed the Belgian frontier, Britain declared war on Germany. In the nine days from 28 July 1914, when Austro-Hungary declared war on Serbia, Germany declared war first on Russia, then on France; Austro-Hungary declared war on Russia, Britain on Germany, and then on Austria. By the first week in November 1914, Japan was at war with Germany and Austro-Hungary and Turkey at war with Britain, France and Russia. All these declarations of war were in accord with treaties signed by the parties concerned. All legal and in order. At least 10,000,000 fighting men were killed and 20,000,000 wounded.

Europe, including the Balkans, at the outbreak of World War I in 1914. The declarations of war were as follows: 24 July—Austria–Hungary on Serbia; 1 August—Germany on Russia; 3 August—Germany on France; 4 August— Germany on Belgium, Britain on Germany; 6 August—Austria–Hungary on Russia, Serbia on Germany; 12 August—France on Austria–Hungary, Britain on Austria–Hungary; 23 August—Japan on Germany; 24 August— Japan on Austria–Hungary; 25 August—Austria–Hungary on Belgium; 2 November—Russia on Turkey, Serbia on Turkey; 5 November—Britain on Turkey, France on Turkey

To tell the story of the outbreak of World War I in terms of international law as it existed in 1914 suggests that this vast and terrible tragedy was caused by a Bosnian revolutionary assassinating an Austrian Archduke. This was far from being the case. Britain did not declare war on Germany for this reason, nor did Germany declare war on Russia and France on this account. It would be mad to suppose that Japan declared war on Germany and Austro-Hungary because of the death of an Austrian prince, no matter how exalted he may have been.

The assassination in Sarajevo in June 1914 was only the spark which set alight an armed conflict of interests among the great states of the world. Such a conflict was nothing new in human history. The only new feature was the immense scope of the conflict and the involvement of whole populations in the tragedy. And it must be borne in mind that World War I was not the first world war. The Seven Years' War in the mid-eighteenth century between Britain and its allies on one side and France and its allies on the other had been fought not just in Europe but in the Americas and in Asia. The Napoleonic Wars at the end of the eighteenth century and during the first fifteen years of the nineteenth had similarly involved fighting around the world and had similarly brought in their train revolutions not just in Europe but in Latin America.

Conflict, as we have suggested in the first chapter of this book, was a feature of politics even in Robinson Crusoe's island, inhabited in the beginning by only one man. And so it has been through history. Cain killed Abel, as we are told in the first book of the Bible: a symbolic rendering of the conflict between hunters and herdsmen, who require for their activities large amounts of land, and agriculturists who live in compact communities and require settled conditions in which animals do not devour everything they can find for food. The celebrated 'Western' movie, *Shane*, retells in a modern setting in nineteenth-century America the Cain and Abel story of the conflict between agricultural farmers and ranchers, and how the conflict was resolved by a gunfight in which Shane, the hired gun of the farmers, won because he was faster, i.e. technically more competent.

The conflicts of interests which came to a head in World War I were not simple conflicts of farmers and ranchers resolved by gunfights between individuals. The participants in World War I were great industrial and trading nations, which controlled vast areas of land and many peoples not only in Europe but around the world. All the major participants, except Austro-Hungary, had territories and people outside Europe which they controlled and which they regarded as their 'possessions', and which in international law were under their sovereign authority. And Austro-Hungary was also an empire, for the Hapsburg emperor in Vienna was not only Emperor of Austria, he was King of Hungary and he ruled over many subjects of Slavic descent such as the Bohemians, whom we know today as Czechs, Slovaks, Galicians, Bosnians and so on.

The great industrial nations of Europe had, by 1914, penetrated and brought under their control nearly all the less technologically advanced communities in the world and in the Far East the non-white, non-European Japanese empire had arisen. For two centuries the Autocrat of all the Russias, the Tsar, had extended his control over vast areas of Asia, bringing under Russian control millions of men and women who were neither Christians nor Slavs.

This long process by which technologically advanced industrial and commercial communities brought under their control peoples whose technologies and economic organisation were less developed than their own can best be illustrated by the case of China. China at the beginning of the nineteenth century was a large and numerous community, and the Chinese have been a civilised people for at least 3000 years. Their art and literature was highly developed and their scientific knowledge was wide-ranging and sophisticated. But theirs was a very conservative society, based upon agriculture and under the administration of a well-organised and elaborate bureaucracy. The Chinese notion of inter-national relations was to have nothing to do with foreigners. On the landward side they built a wall to keep out the barbarians, so long and immense that it is the only manmade structure visible from the moon. Their great cities were protected by sea, and they thought that all they had to do was to prohibit foreigners from entering their ports. When the King of England, George III, sent them an envoy requesting them to open their ports to the British for the purposes of trade, the Chinese government told the envoy that China had everything needed for civilised life, and that they had no desire to enter into relations with barbarians. This was a serious mistake.

The Chinese were the first inventors of what the Europeans call gunpowder. It is symptomatic of their civilisation that the only use the Chinese could think of for this substance was entertainment in the form of fireworks. By the time the Europeans reached China with any hope of defying the Chinese prohibition to their entry, they had had 500 years' experience in killing one another with gunpowder and in the improvement of their means of doing so with muskets, artillery, mines and rockets. The Chinese were, therefore, at a severe disadvantage when the Europeans, and particularly the British, sought to 'open up' China to commerce. The Chinese government wanted to preserve the isolation of China from the barbarians, but they had little military means of doing so, and no industrial base for the development of an army and navy capable of enforcing their determination to remain isolated from foreign influences and foreign commerce.

The result was a series of military defeats starting with the Opium Wars, 1840–42, between Britain and China, which bit by bit forced the Chinese to surrender territory like the island of Hong Kong to the foreigners but, more importantly, to end the prohibition on commerce and to establish the rights backed by force of Britain and France and eventually Germany, Russia and Japan to buy, sell and invest in China. By the time of the revolution which overthrew the Chinese emperor in 1911, China had been divided among the European great powers and Japan into spheres of influence, and it looked as if China would be carved up and parcelled out to the Great Powers in the way India, much of Asia and nearly all Africa had been, and was being, divided up and brought under the control of the sovereigns of Britain, France, Germany, Russia, the Netherlands, Japan, Portugal and Italy.

This partitioning of the non-industrialised world by the industrialised and industrialising nations was a competitive process. Among the nations of Europe it became important and fashionable to have an empire, i.e. territory outside the homeland under the political control of the sovereign of the home country. Even the King of Italy and his government entered the race for empire once Italy became a unified state in 1871. The Italians had to make do with some bits of desert on the shore of the Red Sea, and suffered a stunning defeat when they attempted to take over the ancient, independent empire of Ethiopia in 1896.

The scramble for empire produced much political tension among the European states and between the Japanese government and the Russians and the Chinese once Japan embarked on a course of empire, following the establishment in Japan in the 1860s of a regime determined to modernise rapidly and equip itself with a technologically up-to-date army and navy and the steel and chemical industries necessary to support such a military establishment. France and Britain came close to war on several occasions during the partition of Africa. The old-fashioned Turkish empire, ruled by a priest-king, the Sultan, managed to survive because France, Britain, Russia and, after 1870, Germany could not agree upon how to take the Turkish empire completely apart. As it was, parts of the Turkish empire passed under the control of European states. Egypt, for example, became a semi-independent state controlled by Britain.

It was said about the empires of the nineteenth century that trade followed the flag, i.e. that the Europeans and then the Japanese conquered and occupied territory for commercial reasons. But often the flag followed trade, i.e. the commercial connections with African communities, and indeed with the Chinese, provoked armed intervention overseas in order to protect European traders from interference with their activities and to establish political relations which increased security for trade, investment, the building of railways and the exploitation of agricultural and mineral resources.

Critics of empire in Britain argued that the empire was nothing more than a system of outdoor relief for the British upper class. By this they meant that expansion of the British empire made jobs for soldiers, missionaries and civil servants who controlled and educated 'backward' peoples. This was one view, but it took no account of the fact that large numbers of Europeans of every kind and condition found opportunities for employment overseas as railway-builders, skilled workers, farmers, ranchers and traders. Others argued that the Europeans bore a great burden, 'the white man's burden', carrying civilisation to primitive peoples and to communities like India, Burma and China, which were admittedly civilised but whose peoples were not, it was believed, capable of large-scale industrial and technological organisation. The Japanese, of course, demonstrated that people did not have to be white and European to be up-to-date technologically and militarily.

At the beginning of this chapter we described briefly the immediate events which led to World War I. It should be evident, however, that great developments of enormous complexity brought on the crisis. One of these was the growth in northern and central Europe of a new, large and technologically advanced state, Germany. During the eighteenth century and during the first quarter of the nineteenth century what is now Germany was divided into several states only one of which, Prussia, was of much military consequence. The coming of the industrial revolution based upon the invention and development of heat engines and their use in factories and transport transformed the German community, particularly in the Rhineland, where an iron and steel engineering industry grew up very rapidly from 1840 onwards. In 1870, as a result of the Franco-Prussian war, which deprived France of Alsace and Lorraine, an area with an immense industrial potential, the German community became a unified state, with greater industrial and technological strength than any in Europe. In many branches of endeavour, and especially in science and engineering as well as in music and academic scholarship, Germany led the world. Nothing wrong or dangerous in this.

After the passing of the conservative, old architect of Germany's political transformation into a unified state, Prince Bismarck, German leaders became increasingly ambitious to cut a big figure in the world of international politics and to acquire an empire outside Europe, or possibly in Europe at the expense of Russia. To accomplish this purpose, they believed they needed in addition to their large, well-trained and well-equipped army a technologically advanced navy, which they were well equipped industrially to build. Building a large and powerful navy was a direct challenge to Britain. Britannia ruled the waves around the world, but this meant that its ships were in all the oceans and only some of them were in European waters, where the German navy was developing as potentially the strongest armed force in the North Sea. The British attempted to meet this development by building a great fleet of 'Dreadnoughts', heavily armoured and heavily gunned for service in European waters.

The British did not have a large army, and Britain had never had a system of compulsory conscription of the male population such as existed in the states of continental Europe. Their army was no match in size with the German, French or Russian armies and some doubts as to its competence had been raised by its performance against the Boers in South Africa. But the British Government had always been skilful at gaining allies on the Continent. The circumstances dictated that the British cease standing aloof from continental alliances and the British Foreign Secretary first began to cultivate friendly relations with France and Russia. Second, he promised that if Germany attacked France, Britain would fight in alliance with the French, and French and British soldiers began to plan for this possibility.

Thus, when war came, the greatest industrial power in Europe found itself isolated with only one ally in Europe: Austro-Hungary, which, although industrially strong, had many political problems stemming from the diversity of its population and the incipient nationalism of its many minorities. The intensity of the tragedy of World War I can be attributed mainly to the fact that Germany could not easily be beaten because it was a very strong state industrially, had a large, well-disciplined population and had the enormous advantage of interior lines of communication.

The devastation and death caused by the war and the terrible plague, the Spanish influenza, which followed caused people to believe with good reason that the Four Horsemen of the Apocalypse were abroad in the world. A popular cry went up: 'Never again! Wars must cease!' This was nearly seventy years ago. Since then the world has experienced a worse catastrophe than World War I, and even nation-states anxious to stay out of trouble and on the sidelines of world politics today spend on arms a proportion of their resources which William the Conqueror or Edward I would have regarded as extravagant and unnecessary. George Washington and his contemporary, the Tsarina Catherine the Great, could never have imagined the scale of armaments their

The result of all those declarations of war. Death and devastation at an artillery post at Mont St Quentin in 1918. Twenty-one years later, Europe was at war again

countries maintain in order to balance the power of one against the other.

We can discern two general responses to the misery and loss occasioned by World War I. One was the endeavour to create an international institution with the purpose of settling peacefully international conflicts of interest and reduce and, perhaps, eliminate wars. The other was revolutionary: to break up the empires of the past and to create new nation-states and/or states organised on Marxist lines, which it was believed, would be peaceful because the public ownership of the means of production would eliminate profit-seeking supposed by Marxists to be the cause of war.

Obviously, the foundation of the League of Nations as an international institution dedicated to the peaceful resolution of conflicts among nations, the emergence of new nations from the collapse of the Austro-Hungarian and Turkish Empires and the Marxist revolution in Russia did not eliminate war. None the less these developments changed the world and the international political system. Poland, which had been destroyed as an independent state in the eighteenth century, emerged as a new sovereign state. So did Czechoslovakia and Hungary. A new state of Yugoslavia, which was the former state of Serbia expanded to incorporate lands and peoples of the old Austro-Hungarian empire, came into being. The Turkish empire broke up, and Turkey became a republic, while at the same time parts of it were taken over by the British and the French, who ruled in Syria and Palestine under a mandate from the League of Nations. Several Arab kingdoms emerged, not completely independent of Britain, but not governed directly by any European power. In the Baltic, Finland, Estonia, Latvia and Lithuania threw off Russian control and became independent states. There was a revolt in Ireland which ended in the creation of the Irish Free State, a stage on the road to the creation of the Irish Republic.

The emergence of new nation-states, large and small, gave a great impetus to agitation for national independence, particularly in Asia. The possibility of an independent India began seriously to be considered both by leaders of the Indian community and by the British Government in London, although serious differences developed about when and how national independence would come. German and Russian power and influence were eliminated from China, and the Chinese republican government, established in 1911, began to agitate for the ending of the unequal treaties upon which the presence of the British, French and Japanese in China was based.

Even in the white dominions of the British Empire, which were almost completely independent in matters of domestic politics, there developed especially in Canada, the Union of South Africa and Australia a strong inclination to resist the notion that the British Government made the foreign-policy decisions of the British Empire and that the resources and manpower of these communities were automatically at the disposal of the British Government in any international crisis.

While it is true that the response to World War I did change much, the Treaty of Versailles, which ended the war in Europe, the foundation of the League of Nations and the emergence of new nation-states, did not fundamentally alter the international political order, nor did these developments bring peace. A new and more terrible war broke out in 1939. World War II was in many respects a continuation of World War I on a vaster scale and with more telling consequences as far as the old empires were concerned. There are now no British, Dutch, French or Portuguese Empires.

But did World War II change the international political system? Has the cry 'Never again!' been answered?

The answers given in 1945 were very similar to those given in 1918. Political thinkers and leaders endeavoured to strengthen international law, to outlaw war and to eliminate war as a legitimate means of settling disputes between sovereign states.

The expression of these endeavours after World War I was the League of Nations. The League had a number of serious defects. For example, the largest industrial state in the world, the United States of America, was not a member in spite of the fact that the President of the United States, Woodrow Wilson, was a strong advocate of the League. Nor was the USSR until 1934. Furthermore, the covenant of the League did not outlaw war, nor did the League possess the military means of doing so. In fact, the League was more an aspiration than a reality, and at best a forum in which nations could state a case. The League failed to protect China from Japan and Ethiopia from Italian attack. This failure was the failure of its members, who knew very well that saving China from Japan or Ethiopia from Italy meant a war to stop the aggressors. They were more interested in not going to war than in eliminating war: a serious contradiction. In the years of the League of Nations from 1919 to 1939, the fear of war was so great that bold and ruthless politicians like Hitler, Mussolini and the militarist rulers of Japan found this fear to be their greatest asset in wringing concessions after concessions from the democratic states to the point that they were obliged either to capitulate or fight. Britain and France sought to appease the Fascist dictators, and so did the Soviet Union. Appeasement did not produce peace but war.

After the defeat of the Fascist dictatorships and the capitulation of the Japanese the cry 'Never again!' was heard once more. The victorious allies again sought to reconstruct the international system with the object of eliminating war. The United Nations Organisation was intended as the answer, designed, it was believed, to overcome the defects of the League of Nations.

Unlike the League, the United Nations Organisation was made up of the largest and most powerful states in the world, and was open to all nations willing to subscribe to the founding Treaty which committed the signatories 'to practise tolerance and live together in peace with one another as good neighbours, and to unite our strength to maintain international peace and security, and to ensure, by the acceptance of principles and the institution of methods, that armed force shall not be used, save in the common interest, and to employ international machinery for the promotion of the economic and social advancement of all peoples'.

Obviously, matters have not worked out in the way that those who framed the Charter of the United Nations hoped they might, and those nations who pledged themselves to the Charter have not behaved consistently in accordance with their solemn undertakings. To be fair to the founders of the United Nations, they did not indulge themselves exclusively in wishful thinking. They saw quite clearly that peace and law only became operational and real, as they do in nation-states, by the exercise of power by a sovereign authority which can, when persuasion fails, compel those determined to impose their will on others to desist, to obey the law and to have disputes settled by the judgement of independent agencies such as the International Court of Justice or by arbitrators. In the Security Council of the United Nations the architects of the United Nations attempted to establish an authority possessing the armed force necessary for the exercise of sovereign power. None of the great powers possessing the means for the exercise of sovereign power over the whole world, however, were willing to deliver their power to the United Nations. Instead, the men and women who founded the United Nations created a Council in which each of the great powers would be represented. The Security Council can only exercise sovereign power to enforce international law and prevent armed conflict if the five representatives of the great powers—the USA, the USSR, Britain, France and China—are unanimous and supported by at least two of the six non-permanent members of the Security Council.

In spite of the noble purpose to which the United Nations is committed, its establishment has not changed the essentials of the international political system as it existed before World War I. The working parts of the system are still sovereign states, large and small,

A meeting of the Council of the League of Nations

weak and strong. Each is still in practice the best and final judge of its own interests. There is still no power centre in the world sufficiently strong and authoritative to legislate for, control and judge the whole in the way that the Government of the United States, under its Constitution, is the final authority in the territory of the United States, the Government of the USSR in its territory or the Government of Costa Rica in its territory. The independence of each state in the international community, i.e. the capacity of the state to make its own laws, enforce its own laws and judge its own people, depends upon its capacity to prevent encroachments upon the authority and power of its government. Independence is ensured by force of arms or by diplomacy or by a combination of both. Diplomacy is simply bargaining with friends and enemies alike or with states which are neutral, being neither friends nor enemies.

In the ordinary intercourse of nations, diplomacy figures much more often and continuously than arms, but arms are always in the background as a last resort which, if they fail, presages a partial or total loss of independence. The Swiss Republic has never fought a war for over three centuries, and it is now nearly two centuries since foreign forces traversed Swiss territory. Yet the Swiss maintain a formidable military establishment. Every tunnel, pass and way into Switzerland is mined for destruction in an emergency. Every able-bodied Swiss male is obliged to undergo military training for 113 days in his twentieth year, and to undergo training twenty days a year for eight years and for thirteen days a year every second year thereafter. He is liable for military service until fifty years of age and until fifty-five years of age if an officer. Diplomacy has kept Switzerland free of war longer than any modern nation, but armed force is part of its diplomacy. No nation fears attack by Switzerland, but none of her neighbours dare attack her. The losses in such an attack would be enormous and there would be little left of use to the victors. It should be noted that Switzerland does not belong to the United Nations nor to any international body which takes, or pretends to take, decisions about which its members may quarrel.

The international political system is based theoretically upon the rule that the government of each nation-state ought to mind its own business, and respect the right of all other governments to mind their own business. This rule is expresssed in the act of recognition. In international law, recognition is like admission to a club. It means that the existing members of the club accord to the new member all the rights and privileges of club membership and expect the member recognised to fulfil the duties of membership. In the club of nation-states there is, however, no blackball rule. The objection of one member or even several members cannot prevent other members recognising governments if they wish to do so. Recognition means that a government agrees to treat another government as it would itself wish to be treated, and particularly to regard it as the sovereign authority in the territory in which it exercises power. When one government recognises another, it will, for example, exchange diplomatic representatives such as ambassadors; it will permit citizens to visit back and forth, engage in trade, give each other's citizens the full protection of the law, and in general behave in a civilised way in relations which the state recognised. This does not necessarily mean that by recognition a government approves of everything another government does. The British Government, for example, recognises the Republic of South Africa but this does not mean that the British Government approves of the apartheid policies of the South African Republic any more than its recognition of the Government of the United States before the Civil War meant that it approved of slavery in the United States or, later, that it approved of the apartheid policies of certain states in the southern United States which only ended after the decision of the United States Supreme Court in the case of *Brown* v. *The Board of Education* in 1954 and the Civil Rights Act of 1966. In an ideal world, perhaps, all governments should be able to approve of all other governments, but in the world as it exists, life can only go on by accepting that other people and other governments are different and even bad by one's own standards. Recognition in international law means admission to the international community, which in turn means the acceptance of the minimum standards of behaviour necessary for peaceful intercourse between states and their citizens.

Revolution and profound changes in political values and practices in a community often affect recognition and membership in the international system. The French Revolution and the execution of King Louis XVI of France created a great crisis among the states of Europe, most of which were ruled by monarchs or princes. Could a government which executed a king be recognised? In the end the kings and princes of Europe were obliged to recognise that, whether they liked it or not, a new kind of government existed in France, that the successive revolutionary regimes of France could not be overthrown and that the Directory, the Consulate and the Imperial Government of Napoleon Bonaparte were facts which had to be recognised and so, of course, recognition by some states, and then by others, followed.

A similar process of refusal to recognise, followed by recognition can be observed during and after the Russian Revolution and the Communist rise to power in China.

When World War I broke out all the participants in the war recognised each other, but they were at war with one another, a quite legal activity and an accepted method of settling disputes among nations in the international political system as it existed at that time. But it is a characteristic of war that the participants want to win, and they soon did not mind how. World War I quickly ceased to be a sporting event played according to the rules of war laid down in books on international law. The governments involved sought not just to destroy each other's armed forces but to destroy each other. This happened to such an extent that four of the monarchies—of Austro-Hungary, Germany, Turkey and Russia—which entered the war were destroyed by revolution and in the Russian case the social and economic order, as well as the government, were shattered.

When the fighting ceased (and the Armistice in November 1918 was not the end except in western Europe) it was not at all clear which governments were recognised and by whom. Nor was it clear that recognition of one state by another meant reciprocal respect for the independence of sovereign authority of governments or the social and economic order.

This was particularly so in the case of the Soviet government, which had established itself following the overthrow of the Tsar in 1917. The Soviet authorities regarded as a major weapon in international politics the stimulation of revolutionary activity by the Communist International in all states which they classed as capitalist and bourgeois. They were willing to recognise and be recognised by other states, to exchange ambassadors and engage in trade and a limited degree of intercourse with other states, but they never abandoned the practice of political agitation in other societies and the establishment of secret connections with individuals in positions of influence in other governments, either for the purposes of obtaining information or influencing political decisions. In spite of this new aspect of politics developed by the Soviet government and its agitational apparatus, other governments, some sooner, some later, recognised the Soviet Government. Germany did so in 1922, Britain and France in 1924. The United States did not recognise the USSR until 1933, in spite of the fact that for many years previous to this date American business interests participated in Soviet development on a large scale.

After World War II similar problems of recognition arose. The Communist regime in China was established in 1949, but it was not until 1974 that the Government of the People's Republic of China was recognised by the United States. Although the state of Israel was established in May 1948, as a consequence of a resolution of the General Assembly of the United Nations, and was recognised as an independent state within days of this resolution by the United States and the USSR, no predominantly Muslim state, except Egypt and Iran, has yet (1984) recognised Israel.

From these examples it can be seen that the act of recognition is a political as well as a legal act, and so is non-recognition. Recognition by some but not necessarily all states enables the government of a state to participate in the life of the international community and the citizens of the state enjoy the protection of the law outside the national boundaries, at least in the territories whose governments recognise its government. A citizen of Israel, for example, will not enjoy the protection of the law in Saudi Arabia but will do so in the USSR and the United States.

From the foregoing the reader readily deduces that the international political system much resembles what Hobbes imagined the state of nature to be. If we substituted the word 'state' for the word 'man' in Hobbes' definition of the state of nature, we come up with 'Hereby it is manifest that during the time states live without a common power to keep them all in awe, they are in that condition which is called war; and such a war, as is of every state against every state . . . so the nature of war consisteth not in actual fighting; but in the known disposition thereto, during all the time there is no assurance to the contrary . . .'

Observation confirms this definition. States are armed, and their place in the international political system is determined by their capacity to defend themselves and to attack others. The history of the twentieth century strongly suggests this to be so. The armed collisions of the great states in World War I and World War II wrecked some of them, so that some of the great empires dissolved and many new nation-states emerged from the tragic chaos of war, but the increase in the number of states has not changed the system. Many of the actors are new but the stage and the scenario of the play are the same.

If this is so, why does not the play, as in all tragedies, end in death and destruction? The answer is an open one: it may yet do so.

Since the end of World War II in 1945, the world has not been at peace in any absolute sense of the word. Asia, Africa and the Americas have all experienced wars of varying degrees of intensity and destruction. There is one big fact, however. A war between the great powers has not so far developed. Why?

The answer lies in the balance of power. None of the great powers are sufficiently strong to impose their will on the rest. This does not mean that no great power would wish to do so. The fact is that none can do so, at least for the time being.

There is a further deterrent factor, i.e. the knowledge that an endeavour to do so by armed force will produce such devastation that victory of one over the others will have no meaning, because there will be few people and little productive capacity left in the territories of the combatants. The main beneficiaries, if any, of a third world war of the superpowers will be either the large powers like China, India and Japan, which remain on the sidelines, or the lesser powers, who are wise enough to remain neutral.

Although they are bitterly opposed to each other, the United States and the USSR are dependent upon each other for maintaining their positions in the international political system. Without the antagonisms they feel for each other, the dominant interest groups in each society will lose their *raison d'être*. If they unleash their antagonism they will both be destroyed and, provided anyone survives the effects of nuclear war, Chinese, Indian or even Argentine politicians will take the places of American and Soviet politicians on the world stage.

The polarisation of power in the possession of the United States and USSR has a further effect upon the international system. States of lesser power than the superpowers gravitate towards one or the other of these opposites in formal or informal alliances. This gravitation is motivated by the desire for safety and such independence as alliance with either power will allow. It is further motivated by the hope that through an alliance they may be able to influence the conduct of their mighty friends to maintain peace or to benefit themselves. These are not necessarily compatible purposes.

Not all states follow this policy of gravitation. The location and resources of some states enable them to adopt a 'non-aligned' or neutral position, as Switzerland and Austria do. France, too, has attempted with less convincing consistency than Switzerland to adopt a neutral position *vis-à-vis* the United States and the USSR, and French foreign policy is influenced, it may be supposed, by the existence in France of a large Communist party, with a long record of obedience to the dictates of the Soviet Government.

The balance of power and its ramifications is one factor in the absence of world war. Another, less susceptible to analysis, is the necessity of all communities of co-operating in some way or another by trading with one another, learning from one another, entertaining each other and satisfying curiosity about each other.

These necessities of human co-operation across the boundaries created and maintained by governments are increasingly being met by international organisations having no political character. These bodies make the rules and regulations necessary for the safe, efficient and continuous provision of services of importance to all peoples of the world, irrespective of their race, religion, language, location or social and economic status.

Perhaps the first, and still one of the most important organisations of this kind was established in 1863; at first it was called the International Postal Commission and then from 1878 onwards the Universal Postal Union. Postal services are taken for granted in every part of the world, but it is a minor miracle that a letter put into a pillar box in a hill-village in Wales will be delivered in a matter of days or weeks in the interior of Red China. That this can happen requires organisation of world-wide dimensions, and this is created and the miracle happens without the existence of world government or a world-embracing sovereign power. The postal organisation of any state anywhere can join the Universal Postal Union provided it undertakes to obey the rules and regulations of the Union, which is governed by a small Council representative of members and served by a small staff at the headquarters of the Union in Switzerland. All mail is pre-paid and the postage charges are collected by the post office which accepts the mail. The members undertake to deliver all mail coming into its post offices from other members. Simple rules govern the costs of transport of mail from one member-state to another member-state of the Union, so that in practice there is very little to be paid on balance. All accept the definition of what is mail and how it should be addressed and franked as evidence of pre-payment and of proper origin. If there are any disputes about the rules, these disputes are settled by arbitration within the Union.

There now exist dozens of international organisations which govern telecommunications, aerial transport, health and safety in travel and at work, finance and banking, trade and tariffs, property rights for inventions and cultural creations. Governments can and do sometimes interfere with the work of such international organisations, but they can only do so by imperilling services which they and their citizens need. Landing a heavy aircraft presents the same problems and requires a uniformity of rules governing procedures in the use of a vast array of technical devices in Moscow as it does in Washington; as it does in Harare; as it does in Johannesburg. In a sense technology and its requirements have emancipated many modern activities from the control of governments, and have delivered them into the charge of those who work at providing the services which technology makes possible. This process has not gone sufficiently far for us to suppose that administrative international bodies can and will supersede sovereign states as decisive factors in life.

It must be noticed that these bodies which have an official character and a quasi-governmental status much resemble large, private business interests which have, for most of this century, pursued international financial and commercial policies plainly contrary to the international policies of their governments. It has already been observed that American industrial interests and oil-speculators engaged in very large and important undertakings in the Soviet Union long before the American government thought it prudent and politic to recognise the Soviet Government. The British Government's decision to recognise the Soviet Government in 1924 was very greatly influenced by the desire and need to trade with the Russians as Britain had done for many years before the Revolution. Nowadays, in the 1980s, it is a fact of common knowledge that in spite of the arms race and the almost daily exchange of insults between the American and Soviet Governments and organs of propaganda, the Americans sell, and the Soviets buy, advanced technological apparatus, foodstuffs and consumer goods, and they accept payment directly and indirectly from the Soviets. When this process began, Lenin, who welcomed the willingness of the capitalists to trade with the Soviets, observed that he and his comrades would hang the bourgeoisie with their own rope. By this he meant that economic intercourse would so strengthen Soviet power that in the end it would be able to finish off the capitalist democracies. This has not yet happened, but it is a possibility which does not seem to trouble the business class in the United States and the countries of the European Economic Community. It is one of the strange ironies of politics that some workers' organisations, such as trade unions in the Western democracies, have been, since the Bolshevik takeover in Russia, more anti-Soviet than some business interests, supposed by the Marxists to be the natural and implacable enemies of Communism.

The desire to make money, to produce goods and services, and to buy and sell them, has always been a solvent of political antagonisms and has always worked in the direction of peace and order, and this, for one simple reason: that industry and trade requires peace and order for their pursuit.

The political forces which create and sustain governments, however, tend to work in the opposite direction: towards power and its increase. This, more than any other factor, imparts to the international political system its ambivalent and dangerous character.

While it is true to say that the international system in the 1980s does not differ in principle from the system as it existed before the outbreak of World War I in 1914, it must be kept firmly in mind that much, too, has changed. The United Nations Organisation has not been a conspicuous success as a peace-keeping agency, nor has it contributed much to the lesser objective of keeping down the level of expenditure on armaments. None the less, it does serve as a forum in which the lesser states are able to express themselves and to stir up public opinion against the tendency of the superpowers to act as arbiters of the fate of the world. Just as the existence of representative and responsible government in the real democracies enables interests and points of view to be heard, and to have some effect upon political decision-making, the General Assembly of the United Nations enables the voice of otherwise inarticulate interests to be heard. These voices do not have much direct effect upon the decisions of the superpowers, but the indirect effect is considerable and is a cause of some hope for the future. The superpowers which dominate the Security Council of the United Nations may discredit themselves by the pursuit of their own interests to the point of nuclear disaster, but there is also the possibility that they may not, and in the General Assembly there may be the means of restraining them.

The international political system of the 1980s operates in a rather different milieu than that which existed before 1914. Then the communication of information was slow compared with today, and much of it was presented at second and third hand, usually in a printed form. Today we live in what has been called a 'global village'. Information is almost instantaneously spread throughout the world, and much of the most dramatic and political is visual. The effect of instant communication is not easily predictable, and governments can no longer be sure of public response to their actions. For this reason some governments, and particularly the governments of the pseudo-democracies, make strenuous efforts to suppress, control and manage the flow of information, but this is not always completely successful. As a consequence governments—even the most authoritarian—are not as free as they once were to play the game of international politics unfettered by the influence of any public opinion except their own. In a sense politics has become, or is becoming, more internationalised and democratised. It by no means follows from this that the world is being made a safer or a more orderly place, but it does mean that the international political system is no longer a matter for the governments of nation-states alone.

The present state of affairs in the international sphere differs in another important respect from that which prevailed before 1914. Then the world was divided into great multi-racial, multi-lingual and multi-religious empires on the one hand, and into smaller nation-states which tended to be mainly people of one race, one language and one religion on the other. There were, of course, exceptions like Switzerland, where the people spoke three of the major European languages and were Protestants and Catholics, but it can be said with some truth that the members of the international community before 1914 were either great empires or nation-states of the kind which today we think of as normal, such as France, Britain or Argentina of the 1980s. Today the international community is rather different. The only multi-social multi-lingual empire remaining is the USSR, larger in territory than the Empire of the Tsars but essentially the same in its place in the international community. One of the nation-states of the pre-1914 world which prided itself on its isolation from international politics, and in the superiority of its behaviour on the international political stage, the United States, has become a rival of the USSR as a superpower. Among the lesser nation-states, some of which were once the centres of great empires, there is to be observed a new development: the emergence of regional bodies which range in constitution from loose alliances bound together by some common feature such as being predominently black, or Arabic-speaking or ex-members of an Empire which has passed away to bodies like the European Economic Community, which is a close alliance involving the sharing of sovereign powers in certain activities of governments concerned with economic, financial and cultural concerns.

In addition to these regional or historically-based associations of states, there are inter-state military organisations such as the North Atlantic Treaty Organisation and the Warsaw Pact countries. Before 1939 national armed forces were stationed in peace in the national territories of the sovereign they served. Today the armed forces of NATO are stationed in each other's territory, and particularly in the territory of the German Federal Republic. The Soviet armed forces are stationed in Poland, Czechoslovakia, the German Democratic Republic and in the territory of the other signatories of the Warsaw Pact. The practice of stationing armed forces outside national territories and the stationing there of various types of nuclear rocket installations are a further erosion of the sovereignty of nation-states, and to that extent a serious modification of the international political system.

Additional to these developments is the growing use of clandestine intelligence activities directed towards what is known as the de-stabilisation of political regimes. Before 1914 the governments of nation-states engaged in spying upon one another for the purpose of acquiring information about each other's activities, and conspiracies aiming at the overthrow of rival governments were not unknown. Indeed, as we have seen, such a conspiracy leading to the assassination of the Archduke Franz Ferdinand was the immediate cause of World War I. In the world before 1914, spying and conspiracy were, however, relatively undeveloped and marginal activities in politics. The United States, for example, had no intelligence organisation until World War

II, and such intelligence work as there was was undertaken by the police in the case of domestic political intelligence and by the armed forces purely for battlefield purposes in time of war. Nowadays, intelligence organisations are very large, well financed and wide in the scope of their operations. In the case of the USSR, intelligence activities of the political police, both at home and abroad, are so extensive that the Soviet intelligence community occupies a decisive place in the political process. It is no accident that one President of the Praesidium of the USSR, Yuri Andropov, was an ex-head of the Soviet political police, the KGB.

In the United States the Central Intelligence Agency is a very large organisation operating in all parts of the world. It collects and analyses its own information, and in the first phase of its development enjoyed considerable autonomous power veiled in secrecy. The United States Congress has, however, stepped in to control the CIA, with the result that its activities are now no longer as secret as they used to be, and the prospect of the CIA becoming a parallel government has diminished.

Another difference between the international political system before World War I and the system nowadays has to do with the development of political parties whose activities are not confined to nation-states and directed solely to political participation in constitutional government. The concept of a political party based on class without relation to nation, language and race is of Marxist origin, and took its first form in the First Communist International, which had a brief life during and after the Revolution of 1848 in Germany and France. The notion that a great political party which ignored national frontiers supposed that class feeling was greater than national patriotism. World War I demonstrated that this notion was wrong, and class considerations did not affect the war in its first phase. After the outbreak of the Russian Revolution, the Bolsheviks found that the policies of their enemies could be influenced by political disorders in Germany, France, Ireland and India, and that war-exhaustion and the longing for peace were political factors of advantage to themselves. They at once revived the Marxist notion of an international political party, under their own control, and so the Third Communist International was born.

Before World War I the leaders of sovereign states could conceive of only two ways of dealing with other sovereign states with whom they had differences or who stood in the way of their achieving objectives they had in mind: either they discussed the matter about which they disagreed and, by negotiation, reached an agreement such as a treaty or other form of undertaking, or they declared war on the sovereign or sovereigns with whom they had differences, and the arbitrament of the battlefield determined the terms of the agreement they reached. The

Russian Communists under Lenin's leadership invented a new means of dealing with foreign politicians useful both in peace and in war. This was the Communist International, a political party with branches everywhere in the world, and in which were enlisted the citizens of foreign states. Like the Communist Party in the Soviet Union, the Communist International was a strictly disciplined and highly centralised organisation whose members were trained to do as they were told. Membership in a Communist Party or the Communist International meant abandoning the notion of being a Frenchman or an Englishman or an American or a Hindu and accepting that one's first allegiance is to the working class and its leaders, who are the politicians in charge of the Soviet Government. As the famous Bulgarian Communist, Georgi Dimitrov, said: 'A Communist's first loyalty is to the Homeland of Socialism,' i.e. the USSR.

The Communist International and its successor, the Cominform, became a very useful multi-purpose tool of the Soviet Government. It developed into a vehicle of propaganda on behalf of the Soviet Government, a means of opposing foreign governments on their own ground, a means of infiltrating agents of the Soviet Government into the civil service, armed forces, trade unions and educational institutions; a means of destabilising other governments by promoting strikes in industry and mutinies in the armed forces and, where, as in France and pre-Nazi Germany, the Communist Parties were able to recruit a large following, the means of influencing the legislative and executive processes of government. When civil war broke out in Spain in 1936, the Spanish Communist Party, which was small and powerless, rapidly grew with Soviet assistance to become the dominant force in the Spanish Republic, so much so that Communist commissars killed off the anarchists and socialist republicans and dominated Spain until Franco defeated them and took power.

The use of the Communist International as a tool of the Soviet Government can be illustrated by the behaviour of the Communist Party of Britain. Never a big party like the French Communist Party, the British Communists numbered at the height of their popularity only 30,000 party members, and between 1920 and 1945 elected only 3 members to Parliament. None the less the Communist Party of Great Britain served Soviet purposes very well. When the Nazis came to power in Germany and began seriously to rearm Germany, the Soviet Government became frightened by the possibility that Hitler might seek to found his 'Thousand Years Reich' in eastern Europe. At once, the Communist International was instructed to work for a united front against the Nazis and Fascists. There was nothing wrong with this, because the appeasement of Hitler and Mussolini was as dangerous to the British people as it was to the Soviet Government and the Russian people. But the Communists were not content with advertising the dangers of Fascism. In the climate of opinion which the Communist Party helped to create, the Soviet intelligence and secret police began to recruit Soviet agents to infiltrate the British civil service, armed forces, trade unions, and intellectual establishments. When some of these agents were uncovered it was found that they had disclosed to the Soviet Government much valuable information of a technological, military and political kind.

When the Soviet leader, Joseph Stalin, changed his policy from resistance to the Nazis to one of appeasement, the British Communist Party was at first bemused. When in 1939 the British Government declared war on Nazi Germany in accordance with its treaty obligations to assist Poland if attacked by Germany, the British Communist Party published a pamphlet *How to Win the War*, in which it tried to demonstrate that it knew better than the British Prime Minister, Neville Chamberlain, how to beat the Nazis. Then came a message from Moscow and the Communist International. The line of the British Communist Party changed in a matter of hours. The war for liberty against Fascism became an imperialist war. Strikes were encouraged and organised in industry. Party members were ordered to join the armed forces to conduct anti-war agitation. A front organisation called the Peoples' Convention was developed to disrupt the British war effort. The aim was to transform the imperialist war into revolution.

Then in June, 1941, Hitler attacked the Soviet Union. The imperialist war became overnight a war for democracy. The British Communists once more donned a patriotic garb and called for a more intense war effort, the immediate invasion of German-occupied Europe (the second front) and an indissoluble alliance with the Soviet Union.

The political gyrations of the French Communist Party in response to orders from Moscow matched those of the British Communists. They cheered the war on Germany for a few days, then began to sow disaffection in the industries and armed forces of France. They were a factor in the demoralisation and capitulation of France in the spring and summer of 1940. When Germany attacked the Soviet Union they switched around; French Communists became reistance-fighters and some of them died heroically fighting the German forces of occupation, in the happy but not normal circumstances of being Frenchmen and Communists at the same time. French Communists, like Communists everywhere, were then, as they still are, loyal always to Moscow but to their own nation and its government only when the tactical position of the Soviet Government requires this of them.

When, as a result of severe internal criticisms of their policies in Vietnam, the United States Government decided that it would be prudent and in the interest of the real democracies to attempt to establish friendlier relations with the Communist regimes in the USSR and China and to abate the ideological struggle between the Western democracies and the Communist world, they negotiated an arms control agreement with the Soviet Union. As an aid to the abatement of ideological antagonism an agreement was reached in Helsinki, the object of which was a free exchange of information between the democracies and the Soviet people. The Soviet Government and their dependent states signed the Helsinki agreement but they interpreted the agreement in line with the doctrine of the Soviet leader Brezhnev, which states that 'détente does not in the slightest abolish or alter the laws of the class struggle . . . we make no secret of the fact that we see détente as the way to create more favourable conditions for peaceful socialist and communist construction'.

The expectation that the same criticisms of government policies might develop in the Communist world as had long been the normal practice in the democracies was disappointed. Dissident opinion in the Soviet Union was suppressed and frustrated. Strict censorship continued to be applied. In Poland and Czechoslovakia serious movements of criticism were silenced: in Czechoslovakia by the persecution of critics demanding adherence to constitutional rights and in Poland by the establishment of a military dictatorship and the suppression of the independent workers organisation Solidarity.

It is quite evident that the instrument invented by Lenin to influence and/or destabilise democratic governments and what the Communists call 'bourgeois regimes' has not been abandoned. Its forms and *modus operandi* have been modified to meet changing circumstances, but the two facets of this mode of political behaviour remain:

(1) The utilisation of democratic liberties to subvert democracy; and
(2) The simultaneous organisation of tight controls over the citizens of Communist states so that a minimum of democratic ideas penetrate the iron curtain of Marxist ideology.

6 Politics is about Ideology, Patriotism, Class and Creed

Had we been writing this book four hundred years ago we would have been able to shorten greatly the title of this chapter. Ideology, patriotism and class would have been omitted, for the words had not yet been invented, and creed would have stood alone as the only item on the agenda of politics. Queen Elizabeth I, though she talked often of being English and evoked thereby a warm response in her subjects, thought of herself as first and foremost a Christian, and as the anointed head of the Church of God in England whose first duty was to state and maintain the Apostles' Creed: 'I believe in God the Father Almighty, Maker of Heaven and Earth, and in Jesus Christ His only Son our Lord. . .' By law her subjects were required to appear in Church every Sunday and to say this Creed, and a great many of them actually did so. Today this seems scarcely credible. Only a small minority say the Apostles' Creed. The majority, if asked 'What do you believe?' would give a variety of answers, and many none at all. Some would not even understand the question.

The argument thus far in this book is based on the assumption that men and women are rational creatures who, having natural necessities, set about solving the problems of satisfying them by developing customs, laws and forms of government to keep order and protect their interests. Observation suggests and reasoning confirms that if men and women were only rational creatures they would have but a limited range of political problems, and all of them would in principle be soluble. But observation further confirms that men and women are only rational up to a point, and that reason mingles with feelings to produce beliefs which themselves create political problems.

Let us look briefly at history. When, early in the sixteenth century, the German monk Martin Luther asked and agonised over a purely religious question, 'What shall I do to be saved?' and then came up with answer 'By faith alone', he initiated a movement which changed European society profoundly, converted the Universal Church presided over by the Vicar of God on Earth, the Pope, into a number of independent churches of which the Roman Catholic Church was one of several, opened the way for the unification of power and authority, which characterises modern government, and created the psycho-spiritual foundations of individualism.

In the middle years of the eighteenth century a Swiss political philosopher and educationalist, Jean-Jacques Rousseau, argued that the authority of government rests, and can only rest, on the General Will, which is created by custom, habit, prolonged experience of social intercourse and public opinion. Rousseau did not invent nationalism, but he was the first to observe nationalism as a strong political force, and he developed the language and grammar by which it could be discussed. The force of nationalism has grown steadily during the nineteenth and twentieth centuries as more and more aspirants to power have learnt its vocabulary and preached its virtues. The General Will of particular peoples has dissolved all the European empires except the Russian, and even in the land of the Tsars, their successors, the Communist Party, have learned to use the rhetoric of nationalism and adjust to its logic.

In the mid-nineteenth century two German intellectuals, one the grandson of a rabbi and the other a businessman, Karl Marx and Frederick Engels, conceived of mankind as a species divided into classes struggling with one another in an evolutionary process which, they prophesied, would produce a heaven on earth. This they labelled Communism. Marxism has taken root in modern society as a faith which moves mountains, provokes wars and creates tyranny. Heaven remains far off.

Salvation, the General Will and the Class Struggle are but evocative words. Hobbes believed that political understanding depended upon the discovery of truth—another word. 'Seeing,' he wrote, 'that truth consisteth in the right ordering of names in our affirmations, a man that seeketh precise truth had need remember what every name he uses stands for, and to place it accordingly, or else who will find himself entangled in words, as a bird in lime twigs, the more he struggles the more belimed. . .'

And so 'truth consisteth in the right ordering of names' does it? Who can say what the names are and what it the right ordering of them?

Hobbes, who learned much about natural science from Galileo, was one of the first political philosophers to believe that what politics is about and how political forces operate can be discovered by using the procedures of science, i.e. by defining one's terms, using these terms consistently and uniformly and reasoning about them mathematically. Let us do this, and what do we get? What this book so far is: a description and a few analytical insights, and nothing more. And a habit

(*Left*) Friedrich Engels (1820–95) and (*right*) Karl Marx (1818–83), the founding-fathers of Communism

of mind which prompts one to say of salvation, the General Will and the Class Struggle, that they are but 'evocative words'. This is a mistake.

Yes, they are evocative words, but what do they evoke and why? Observation shows that the evocative words of Martin Luther found a response in the society in which he lived. So has the concept of the General Will. So has the notion of the class struggle. The words cannot therefore be dismissed. Politics is also about ideas, or, to use a modern term, ideology.

The words, ideas and ideology are not, however, interchangeable. One can have ideas about anything. An ideology is a system of ideas about men and women in society; about their relations with one another; about goals. Ideologies are themselves factors in politics, for men can forget the interests which serve their material necessities and concentrate their attention on winning struggles over ideas. And they can do the reverse: employ ideology to mask their interests. Hobbes was being quite impractical and wanting in realism when he supposed that all man has to do to order life better is to get the definitions right and use them consistently and logically. Of course, men and women ought to try to be accurate and consistent and logical, but it does not follow that they can be or want to be. Being scientific is like being good; it is often difficult, or boring or beyond human capacity. It may even be counter-productive and self-defeating.

Religion and ideology have much in common. Both require an act of faith on the part of the believer. Faith, according to St Paul, is 'the substance of things hoped for, the evidence of things not seen'. This is as good a definition as any, and it applies across the board to religion and to ideology. There is, however, a difference in the faith which underlies religion and that upon which ideology rests.

Religion—any religion—rests upon the assumption that the unknown and the unknowable constitute a much greater part of the universe than the known and predictable, and that the unknown and the unknowable are more powerful than men and women. Ideologies, on the other hand, rest upon the assumption that man either does know or can be confidently expected to discover a significant proportion of the workings of the universe and can justify the title which V. Gordon Childe, a Marxist anthropologist, once gave to a book, *Man Makes Himself.* God did not make man; man made God, as Marx argued in his youth and continued to believe.

The practitioners of religion and ideologies both assert that they have knowledge. The knowledge they have differs in its origins, but it is knowledge which becomes operational if sufficient numbers of people share the knowledge and believe it to be true. When Macbeth encountered the witches they purported to have knowledge which he did not have. They told him he would be King of Scotland, in much the same way as some American journalists told General Douglas MacArthur he would be President of the United States. The witches' methods of acquiring this knowledge were more preposterous than those of the American journalists, but the knowledge they imparted was the substance of things hoped for, and was believed on that account. Unfortunately, King Malcolm was more trusting and less tough than President Truman, and he met an unhappy demise, whereas General MacArthur was obliged to retire from the United States Army on a pension and nourish himself on the consoling thought that old soldiers never die and many of them do not become Presidents of the United States.

It may be argued, of course, that Macbeth got his information from the wrong kind of people. It is unlikely that Shakespeare was seeking to make the point that, had Macbeth relied upon the knowledge of a Christian bishop and not upon witches, he could have avoided his sticky end. Certainly, a Christian bishop, who took his duties seriously, would have warned Macbeth about too much ambition, would have absolutely excluded murder as a means of mounting the throne of Scotland and might even have pointed out that Macbeth had no legal claim to supreme authority in Scotland. The bishop's advice would have been based upon a knowledge of the mind of God in the matter of human conduct and upon a firm, unquestioning belief in the existence and power of God the Almighty.

Shakespeare was in many respects a thoroughly modern man. Indeed, he had a prophetic capacity which enabled him to anticipate the character of the future. In particular, he was profoundly interested in politics. More than half his plays concern politics, and all of them on political themes, save *Henry V*, are tragedies. For Shakespeare in his depiction of politics God was dead, and no knowledge of God's guidance influenced the struggles for power his plays present. Julius Caesar and Richard III were both uninfluenced in anything they did by the inhibitions to human behaviour which are conveyed to man by the messengers from the divine powers. And all ended up dead, not from natural causes but from political acts. Even the lovers, Romeo and Juliet, fell victims of political antagonisms unchecked by knowledge of God's will and ordinances. As far as politics was concerned, Shakespeare seems to have come to pretty much the same conclusions as Hobbes, and he offered no way out. The elder Hamlet is murdered. The prince Hamlet slays the usurper and is himself slain. Fortinbras has Hamlet's 'dying voice', and with his soldiers Hamlet's successor bears off the bodies of the dead. A shrewd picture of politics without religion or ideology, and none the worse on that account.

There is perhaps a clue to something important in the fact that a man of Shakespeare's genius wrote about politics so extensively without giving to the Christian or any other religion a serious place either as a restraining or energising force in the lives of the kings, queens, princes, emperors, consuls and generals who people his political plays. There is a separation in politics between what men do and what they say. Shakespeare was concerned with what they did, and what motivated them in this. Claudius, Brutus, Titus Andronicus, Lear, Warwick, Richard III and all the others ensnared in struggles for power were motivated by a variety of passions; ambition, lust, vanity, vengeance, jealousy, indecision, pride, and they trod the dusty road to death. Religious beliefs never seriously influenced anything they did.

If we move forward in time to survey the political tragedies of our own day can we say that ideology has ever seriously affected political behaviour? Lamentably, the answer is yes. Shakespeare's political men and women did nothing more than ignore the divine knowledge available to them. We, however, actively embrace our scientific and pseudo-scientific knowledge. Adolf Hitler, for example, developed an extreme form of nationalist ideology and persuaded himself and others that the Germanic peoples were a unique and superior people. Contrary to rational self-interest as well as to ordinary humane consideration for the species, *homo sapiens*, which the major religions inculcate as a sentiment given by God and mandatory for all men and women, Hitler and the leaders of the National Socialist German Workers' Party organised the slaughter on a comprehensive scale of Jews and gypsies, and through purposeful administrative indifference brought about the deaths of millions of Russians and other Soviet citizens taken prisoners of war.

Lenin was a Marxist ideologue. He could not think or feel beyond the limits of his ideas. Bolshevik power was all that mattered. To keep power he did not hesitate to organise a system of terror which wiped out whole strata of Russian society. Lenin and his chief of police, Dzerzinsky, himself a Polish aristocrat, murdered a significant proportion of the aristocracy and the administrative and officer class and the leaders of the peasants and industrial workers. His successor, Stalin, improved on this. He liquidated the kulaks, which is a euphemism for the murder of at least 12 million Russian and Ukranian farmers. Then he murdered a high proportion of his colleagues in the Communist Party and he decimated the officers of the Soviet Armed Forces.

An early photograph of Mao Tse-tung, taken in Yenan during the Sino–Japanese war in 1938

Vladimir Ilyich Lenin (1870–1924)

Mao Tse-tung was another Marxist ideologue who repeated in China what was accomplished by Lenin and Stalin in the Russian Empire. Another Marxist ideologue, Pol Pot, has destroyed the capital city of his own nation, and murdered a high percentage of its inhabitants. Fidel Castro, another professed Marxist, has been somewhat less murderous than his exemplars in Europe. He has murdered and imprisoned only a sufficient number to induce about 15 per cent of the Cuban population to flee the country and thus ensure that he has for the time being no political opponents.

Ideologically motivated mass murder has no rational purpose except the getting and keeping of power. It has weakened and debilitated every society where it has been practised. Shakespeare's tragic heroes confined their murderous activity to the ranks of a small élite. The Fascists and the Communists have democratised political murder, and always for the best of reasons provided by their ideologies.

Ideologies play an important secondary role in the political life of the pseudo-democracies. In the real democracies a variety of ideologies and religions flourish, and some of these provide motives for political action and are often factors in the differences and political struggles for power and influence which distinguish the real from the pseudo-democracies. In the pseudo-democracies the politicians in office want to stay there permanently like royal families, but royal families with real power. Permanency of power requires the absence of effective opposition. One method of reducing and eliminating opposition is to establish uniformity of thought and responses in the subjects of government. Ideology plays an important part in this, because an ideology is a set of beliefs, and the implantation of beliefs is one of the first tasks of education.

One of the presidents of the USSR, Kalinin, put this very bluntly. 'In my opinion,' he wrote, 'education is the definite, purposeful and systematic influencing of the mind of the person being educated in order to imbue him with qualities desired by the educator' (*On Communist Education*, Foreign languages Publishing House, Moscow, 1940). Censorship of all communication is another means of thought control. Ideology provides the standard of what must be taught and what can and cannot be said or written.

The relationship between ideology and the actual policies of governments in the pseudo-democracies is not easy to define or analyse. The ideology, German National Socialism, developed by Adolf Hitler and his Nazi colleagues was an absurd pot-pourri of racial prejudices, sexist nonsense, a credulous belief in big government, a glorification of military violence and a doctrine of German imperialism. At first, this ideology provided the rationale for the destruction of real

The two dictators meet for the first time. Hitler and Mussolini in Venice in 1934

democracy in Germany and the suppression of all political opposition by killing some and imprisoning many in concentration camps. As far as the German economy and welfare policies were concerned, Hitler's government was rather successful. The large public expenditure on armaments, the large-scale programme of public works and the improvement of welfare services served to revive the German economy and put an end to unemployment. In fact, the Nazi Government was extremely popular on account of the domestic peace and prosperity it brought about. In the end, however, the Nazi ideology became the basis of the foreign policy of Germany: a policy of aggressive war against all Germany's neighbours and the use of violence on a vast scale to conquer territory and enslave peoples whom the Nazi ideologists argued were inferior because they were non-German. The criminal insanity of the ideology was revealed, and in the last stages Hitler and his party demonstrated that they were independent of all German institutions, even the most prestigious, and that bishops, cardinals, scientists, business leaders and officers of the armed forces counted for nothing in the determination of government policy. Germany went smash.

German National Socialism and Italian Fascism were extreme examples of nationalism as an ideology, and, it can be argued, are not representative of nationalism as a mode of political thinking. There is something in this argument insomuch as patriotism and nationalism have a 'natural' quality about them which Rousseau observed as a characteristic of the General Will. Culture, language, race and religion are social bonds which create an identity which people can recognise in themselves and which mark them off from other human groupings and geographical areas where other languages and other customs can be observed. It is not surprising, therefore, that people came to believe that a community having an identity of its own ought to be governed by people who belong to the community and have characteristics which the community can recognise as similar to their own. The argument can be carried further. The members of the community ought to participate in creating the government, if for no other reason than ensuring that the government will understand the community and respect and cherish its characteristics.

Because nationalism and patriotism involves a strong element of respect for community characteristics it is easy for this respect to become the glorification of the self by glorifying the nation and attributing to it superiority over others. This tendency became pathological in the case of the German National Socialists, and was carried to such absurd lengths that it isolated Germany and antagonised and frightened the rest of mankind. All of this ended in disaster for the German people.

The social sentiment which we call nationalism has played a large part in the development and dissolution of empires. The British, for example, became very proud of themselves, and they had much to be proud of. They valued what they did as discoverers, inventors, traders and architects of representative and responsible political institutions. As their power and interests arc and the world grew, they came to believe that they had a mission to govern and reorganise the people and places where their activities carried them and from which they could eliminate rivals. God saved the King and He frustrated the knavish tricks of the King's enemies. Britannia ruled the waves and a jolly good thing, because this meant the end of piracy on the high seas and security for trading, colonising, missionary work and the establishment of modern civilisation in primitive and backward places.

But other people had feelings too. They often welcomed what the British had to offer, but they also loved and respected what they themselves had. Counter-nationalism developed in India, Burma, China and eventually in Africa. Even in the areas where British people had settled overseas in large numbers, new, local, self-assertive identities arose, as they did in Australia, Canada, New Zealand and South Africa. This happened, too, very close at hand in Ireland. Nationalism became, therefore, a political solvent of empire just as it was a phase in the creation of empire. What can be observed in the history of the British Empire happened also in the French, Dutch and Portuguese Empires. It can also be observed at work in the American spheres of influence around the world.

The psychological foundations of nationalism are deep and strong, and for this reason politicians in both the real democracies and the pseudo-democracies find it advantageous to flavour their appeals for support with patriotism. Dr Samuel Johnson once remarked: 'Patriotism is the last refuge of the scoundrel.' By this he meant that patriotism from the lips of a politician is frequently employed to obscure other purposes which the politician has in mind. When one hears a policy described as un-English or un-American, one is bound to be wary and sceptical. Nevertheless, nationalism is a serious and abiding factor in politics. In the modern world the state as a product of the General Will is, perhaps, the best easy explanation of the division of the world into 175 nation-states. Even 'universalist' ideologies like Marxism have found in nationalism a stumbling-block on their path to world revolution, and one of which they have to take account.

In the 1930s the extreme nationalism of German National Socialism and Italian Fascism was dramatically confronted by another ideology which today looms large in the world: Marxism. Unlike Fascism and Nazism, Marxism is an intellectually serious ideology which has grown out of several religious and philosophic tendencies in Western European thought. Like Hobbes' thinking, Marxism can be classified as a materialist and scientific *weltanschauung*, or world outlook. It transcends national boundaries and racial divisions, and analyses mankind as a species and not a collection of linguistic and racial groups. Marxists further regard the history of mankind as an evolutionary process characterised by change and measurable progress. Marx and Engels took a lively and critical interest in the analytical work of the great economists of the eighteenth and nineteenth centuries. Into all of this they injected a strong prophetic element characteristic of the Judeo–Christian religious tradition. Finally, they held in rational contempt all the accepted and well-established institutions of the society in which they lived: the family, the churches, property, social conventions and the nation-states. If there is anything wrong anywhere, if anyone feels aggrieved about anything, a Marxist can sooner or later offer a high-sounding general and rational explanation and a revolutionary political cure.

Marxism is now the official ideology of 1½ billion people. This means that Marxism is taught in the schools, is the official and required belief-system of anyone active in political life and for all but a small number of officials of government and officers of the armed forces.

It is instructive to examine why this is so, and why the possessors of power in the Communist world find in Marxism a guide to what to do and a justification for what they do.

In the first place, Marxism is purported to be scientific. This is a fundamental dogma of Marxism. 'Just as Darwin discovered the laws of evolution in organic nature, so Marx discovered the laws of evolution in human history.' So declared Engels in his funeral oration at the graveside of Karl Marx. Lenin was equally dogmatic: 'The Marxist doctrine is omnipotent because it is true.'

Unfortunately Marx, Engels and Lenin did not understand much about science. The natural sciences are a body of analytical procedures, and not a body of facts such as the information in a telephone directory. The hypotheses about evolution advanced by Charles Darwin in *The Origin of the Species* published in 1859 are not true in the light of modern biological knowledge. Nobody 'knows' what the truth is in this matter, and modern palaeontologists are more puzzled by what is as yet inexplicable about evolution than they are impressed by what Engels supposed was true about Darwin's hypotheses.

But the dogma that Marxism is scientific and is therefore true has its political uses. It is supposed by Marxists that in the natural sciences there are always sole solutions to problems. Alternatives to the 'true' solution are mistakes. Marxism as a branch of the natural sciences yields 'true' solutions to social and political problems. There is one solution and none other. The greatest Marxist–Communist of his time is the authoritative scientist of his time, and he therefore knows what the true solutions of problems are. Alternative solutions are unscientific, opportunist, deviationist and anti-Marxist. In short, alternative solutions are heretical. They must be suppressed. Hence the bitterness of the fights inside the Communist parties and Marxist organisations: Lenin against Kautsky, Stalin against Trotsky, Mao against Lin Piao in China, Foster against Browder in the United States, the Spanish Communists against the Trotskyist POUM during the Spanish Civil War. None of the differences were resolved by experimental work in a laboratory. The differences between Stalin and Trotsky were resolved by firing-squads, and Trotsky died in exile; the victim of an assassin who finished him off with an ice-pick in the head. So much for science in Marxist politics.

But mistakes do occur in Marxist states. Khruschev, who succeeded Stalin, the great scientific Marxist and ruler of the Soviet Union, revealed that Stalin's policies had ruined Soviet agriculture, that he had killed several million agriculturalists, and that Russia, which at one time was a very large exporter of food, was from time to time afflicted with famine. The mistakes, however, were blamed on Stalin, not on the science of Marxism. Marxism is sacred, although some of the High Priests are not.

The political significance of this dogma about Marxism as science is the identification it seeks to establish between a political party and its leaders and real scientists and engineers whose procedures of enquiry and analysis *do* yield reliable information which people trust because they can see and experience the results of scientific enquiry and technological developments based upon it. Marxism is, however, more like witchcraft than science, and its political exponents rely upon repetition and incantation and the suppression of critical enquiry in order to sustain its acceptability.

The famous Russian intellectual, Alexander Solzhenitsyn, whom the Soviet Government expelled from the USSR after keeping him in a labour camp for many years, claims that the only people who take Marxism seriously in his native country are those ambitious to make careers in the ruling class and to enjoy its privileges. The mass of the people, according to Solzhenitsyn, are indifferent or hostile to the official ideology. Events in Poland suggest that little credence is given to Marxism there. The heavy censorship which exists where Marxism is the orthodox official creed suggests that those who benefit from it are not very confident of its reliability as a belief-system if exposed to critical analysis.

And yet in the real democracies, in Latin America and the new nations of Africa and Asia, Marxism enjoys considerable popularity, and the agencies of the Soviet Government still use this ideological tool to recruit support for the achievement of their goal prophesied by Marx: Communism. In the universities, schools, churches, trade unions and the professions there are to be found many believing Marxists. Marxism is an intellectual industry in the real democracies, so much so that old publishing firms with traditional conservative affiliations and responsible reputations find it profitable to publish large numbers of books about various aspects of Marxism.

The contradiction of the appeal of Marxism to those ambitious for office and power and its rejection by those who experience in their daily lives the administrative and political control by its exponents requires some explanation. Put briefly, Marxism is an intellectual device for arousing and expressing discontent, but it is a hopeless intellectual instrument for the production of social wellbeing.

Marx made many errors in his economic analysis. For example, he assumed that all work is the same, and wages are determined by the time spent at work without account being taken of skill and experience. Nothing matters to a capitalist except that a worker works longer than the time it takes to produce what the worker consumes. This is the source of profit, and out of profit the stock of capital is created in a money form. This capital is used to purchase more labour time in an endless process, with the result that capital accumulates and the workers become poorer and poorer. All this is logical enough, but the process Marx described bears little resemblance to anything which has happened and is happening in capitalist societies. The workers have not become poorer and poorer. They have become richer and richer in terms of food supplies, housing accommodation, transport facilities and general welfare. Whenever free capitalist enterprise has operated even for short periods of time men and women have begun to live longer, grow taller and enjoy more leisure. Faced by the devastation produced by 'war-Communism' from 1917 to 1921, Lenin was forced to introduce something he ironically called 'the new economic policy', i.e. free enterprise. This produced some improvements in the Russian economy, so much so that Stalin was obliged in the interests of Marxist ideology to destroy free enterprise once again, slaughter a large number of free-enterprise peasants, enslave a large number of people in labour camps and inaugurate a planned economy.

There is another fatal flaw in the Marxist analysis of society. Marx took over from the contemporary economists of Victorian society the notion of self-interest as expressed by Adam Smith and Jeremy Bentham and, as he did with most ideas, he radicalised them and carried them to their absurd logical end. Both capitalists and workers were moved by self-interest, but in opposite directions. From this, Marx deduced the concept of the class struggle. The workers could never improve their lot. Therefore self-interest would prompt them to co-operate together to conquer their enemies, the capitalists, and they would do so, thus producing the Communist Revolution. Again, nothing resembling this has happened in any capitalist society. Self-interest has prompted workers to co-operate with each other either to create agencies, such as trade unions, for more effective bargaining with capitalists or for the creation of enterprises like co-operatives for the marketing and/or production of goods and services for themselves or for insuring themselves against unemployment, sickness and the cost of death in their families. Nor have workers abandoned their allegiance to the nation-states in which they live in favour of the 'international brotherhood of man'. And finally, workers in general have been extremely dubious about the growth of state power along Marxist lines; much more, in fact, than business interests, which have never hesitated about doing business on advantageous terms with Marxist regimes.

The reader cannot understand Marxism and its place in politics if he or she assumes that it is a social science. It can best be understood as an atheistic form of religion. The Marxist account of human history contains within it the prophecy of its outcome, and that outcome is a paradise here on earth. The great prophets of Marxism are sanctified and glorified. Pilgrims file past the tomb of Lenin and gaze upon his embalmed remains. In China everyone starts the day with a reading from the Marx scriptures—currently the works of Deng Hsiao-p'ing, just as they used to be *The Thoughts of Chairman Mao*. In North Korea they sing hymns in honour of Kim Il Sung, and readers familiar with the Christian tradition will recognise the original source of 'The Blessed Diamond':

Marshall Kim Il Sung is our diamond
In him we hide, in him we learn,
A shelter in the time of storm,
Secure whatever ill betide,
A shelter in the time of storm.

O rock divine, O refuge dear
A castle in the time of storm,
Be thou our helper ever near,
A shelter in the time of storm.

Perhaps the most telling testimony to Marxism as an atheistic religion is that provided by the leading American Marxist, Michael Harrington. Writing in a free capitalist society, where it has been impossible to suppress knowledge of the murderous character of controversy among Marxists and the criticisms made by historians, scientists and philosophers, Harrington has attempted to preserve the purity of Marxist theory from those who use it for worldly purposes. Even Marx himself is not spared. Harrington writes:

> Both Marx and Engels thus contributed to the distortion of Marxism, the former on occasion, the latter more systematically. But if these misstatements were, particularly in the case of Marx, only episodic and counterbalanced by a huge corpus of intellectual work that puts the matter rightly, why has the false coin of Marxism been so widely accepted and the genuine treasures all but ignored?
>
> So for most people the first step in grasping the new and future Marx is to forget everything they have heard or read about Marx. At the same time they must accept one of history's strangest ironies: that Marx and the Marxists made a major contribution to the misunderstanding of Marxism (*The Twilight of World Capitalism, a Marxian Epitaph* New York, 1976, p. 28).

Presumably Harrington is now the custodian of the eternal flame of Marxist truth.

In the real democracies one encounters a variety of ideologies and religious creeds. The plural use of these words is significant. In none of the real democracies is there an orthodox ideology or religion. Orthodoxy and real democracy are contradictions. Democracy supposes that individuals and groups freely express themselves and engage in such activities as seem best and most advantageous to themselves. Among these activities is the quest for political office and such power as the constitution of the nation-state allows in the offices sought. In the pursuit of office the aspirants are obliged by the circumstances of election to find some means of recruiting a political following willing to work for them and vote for them. One of these means, but not the exclusive one, may be the preaching of an ideology or identification with a religious creed. The fact that some aspirants to public office adopt these means of recruiting supporters does not preclude others from doing the same or resorting to other means of persuading people to support them. The rules of the game in a real democracy are fixed by the constitution and by such legislation as may be passed from time to time to elaborate the rules and ensure what is believed to be fair play. Those who express a Marxist ideology enjoy the same rights and opportunities as other aspirants to office and power. The principal reason why Marxists have never been able to achieve permanent and exclusive power, as they have done in the pseudo-democracies, has been their inability to win sufficient support to dominate operational constitutional processes, designed to permit the expression of all views and interests.

Ideologies and religious creeds occupy a secondary place in the politics of the real democracies. They serve as a means at best of recruiting the membership and or organising political parties. It can be observed in the real democracies that too much dependence on an ideology is a handicap rather than an advantageous tool in the contests for office and power which are the central features of their political life. The British Conservative Party, for example, which is the oldest and most successful political organisation in the United Kingdom, has no ideology. Membership in the British Conservative Party is achieved by joining a party organisation in the constituency where one lives, and this involves paying a subscription, often determined by the party member himself or herself. There are no articles of belief to which a member must subscribe, and, therefore, there is no Conservative orthodoxy. No-one can confidently say what a Conservative is except that he or she subscribes to the Party and votes for it if so inclined. While it is unlikely that one will encounter in the British Conservative Party anyone who advocates the overthrow of the monarchy and the British Constitution, one will find in the Party a very wide range of views on every imaginable subject, a great variety of interests and a very mixed body of supporters in terms of wealth, social origins and local loyalties. As a result, Conservative aspirants to office in local and national government are a much more mixed bag than their opponents suppose and allege. All that can be said of the British Conservatives is that their political strategy of eschewing ideology works pretty effectively as a means of winning elections, particularly in England as distinct from Scotland, Wales and Ulster.

Since World War I the most successful opposition to the Conservative Party has been the Labour Party. It is a more ideological party than the Conservatives and many of its supporters profess a belief in socialism and, in recent years, Marxism. But from its first beginnings the Labour Party has appealed for support by professing an interest in the wage-workers, who are a very numerous body of voters, and by depending heavily for money and support from the trade unions. On balance, however, the British Labour Party has never regarded the achievement of power as an irreversible process, and the Labour leaders have supported the principles and practices of the British Constitution. This has been wise in terms of their own interest, because the people to whom they make their principal appeal have not markedly exhibited the characteristics of the working class as Marx supposed them to be. British wage-workers, for example, have long exhibited a preference for patriotism rather than internationalism. They have tended to be suspicious of monopolies of power, whether that of employers or government or trade union bosses, and they have long understood the connection between the success of industrial enterprises and their own interest in improved wages and conditions of employment. This last factor helps to explain why in recent years wage-workers have begun transferring their support from the Labour Party to the Conservative Party or to the Liberal or Social Democratic Parties. The Labour Party has become too much concerned with the policies of planning, public ownership and other socialist measures, and has by that means diminished British productivity and adversely affected real wages by the inflation consequent upon high public expenditure on non-productive or badly organised productive activity. They have been alienated, too, by the pacificism strong among middle-class intellectuals in the Labour Party, which they see as a surrender to Communism.

In the North American democracies ideologies have little or no place in political life. Religion is excluded from political contests by the American Constitution. In Canada attempts made by the British Government to establish an official religion in the British colonies failed very largely because religious denominations were many, and to associate the government with one denomination rather than another created more political problems than it solved. The policy of giving to the Roman Catholic Church in Lower Canada (the province of Quebec) a power to tax its adherents did not in the long run contribute to that unification of political support for authority and power, which is one of the purposes of an officially sponsored creed.

Secular ideologies such as Socialism, Marxism, Communism and Fascism have found no place in American politics. In Canada, a class-based socialist party, the New Democratic Party, has enjoyed some success at the level of provincial politics and has exercised some influence in federal politics—particularly in the dominant Liberal Party—but the Socialism of the New Democratic Party is a very watered-down version of Socialist ideology as it has been understood in Europe.

Neither of the great political parties of the United States is in any way ideological. Both the Democratic and Republican Parties resemble the

British Conservative Party inasmuch as their main preoccupations are with winning elections by attracting to themselves as much and as various support as possible. Until President Lyndon Johnson gave a lead in sponsoring civil rights legislation, the object of which is to end racial segregation in the United States, the Democratic Party, of which he was the leader, had long been the party of popular rights, social welfare and trade-union privileges while at the same time the principal agency for segregationist policies of apartheid in the ex-slave states in the American South. Apartheid policies in the South and popular welfare policies in the North were both vote-getters in the areas where they were preached and practised, and therefore they were Democratic Party policies.

A similar lack of ideology can be observed in the Republican Party. It is popularly supposed with some reason to be the party of big business and free enterprise, but the Republican Party has never been a conspicuous friend of free competition and free-market economics. During the long period from the Civil War in the 1860s until the great depression of the 1930s, the Republican Party was a dominant element in American federal politics. During that period the Republicans had the very wide support of American industrial workers and farmers because they sponsored and implemented high tariffs designed to limit foreign competition in American markets to the supposed advantage of American industry and agriculture.

From the moment when the Marxist revolutionaries took power under Lenin's leadership in Russia, there developed in the United States a strong vein of anti-Communism. It was as if the Americans sensed a great ideological challenge to liberal–democratic institutions. This sentiment of anti-Communism, however, never developed into a pervasive ideology which politicians could employ as a means of controlling the subjects of government. Here and there and now and then, politicians like Martin Dies and Senator Joseph McCarthy mounted anti-Communist crusades as a means of whipping up political support for themselves and putting their opponents on the defensive. Richard Nixon made his early reputation as the man who exposed the Soviet spy, Alger Hiss, and he seems to have completely alienated Fidel Castro by implying that he was a dupe of the Communists at a time when Castro's mind was not yet made up about his political orientation, but Nixon as President was anything but intransigently anti-Communist. His successor in the office of the Presidency, Gerald Ford, refused to meet the leading Soviet dissident, Alexander Solzhenitsyn. President Eisenhower was never anti-Soviet, and when he had the choice of condemning the Anglo–French–Israeli assault on Egypt in 1956 and/ or condemning and resisting the Soviet assault on Hungary, Eisenhower condemned and obstructed the Western Europeans and their Israeli allies and washed his hands of any involvement in helping the resistance of central European democrats to Soviet imperialism. It is possible to argue that, in spite of deep antagonisms, the superpowers support each other in the presence of a threat to their power by the third force of lesser powers.

The thrust of this argument is to suggest that ideologies are subordinate to considerations of power. Marxist ideology in the USSR is a means of political conditioning of the subjects of government. In the American case the absence of ideology is a necessary consequence of its well-established liberal constitutionalism. Some are tempted to believe that this absence of ideology is a weakness and that this lays the United States open to penetration by the Marxists. There may be some short-term disadvantages in an open liberal approach to political questions, but in the long run the liberal political system of the United States has great strength, and not least in its appeal to those vast numbers of people who suffer from the malfunctioning of societies governed by people in ideological blinkers.

In the pseudo-democracies where ideological parties dominate the political processes, elections mean nothing. They are a contrivance for publicly confirming the power and authority of the government. They are democratic rituals, and not real events with an influence upon policy-formation and a means by which interests in society find a place in the bargaining process necessary for the co-operation of various elements in socio-economic life. The politicians in the pseudo-democracies are not obliged to appeal to the electorate in terms of a variety of interests which the citizens have as aspects of their real lives producing, thinking and creating.

It is otherwise in the real democracies. Politicians have to be elected in circumstances of choice and competition. The politician in a democracy asks the citizens to do something for him or her, i.e. at least to vote for the politician and perhaps to ask others to vote likewise and even to subscribe to the funds necessary to pay for organising, advertising, canvassing and other aids to the recruitment of support. What can the politician do for the voter? The politician can promise the voter good government. Few voters actually want bad government, and so a promise as general as this has little meaning. The aspiring politician has to make promises of performance in government which have some significance to the voter in terms of the voter's own life, activity and interest. This meaning for voters can and does vary enormously, from vulgar personal bribery to the most altruistic and intellectually sophisticated concern for the public good.

The world depression of the 1930s produced a very great change in the politics of the real democracies. Some of them perished in the depression. Germany and Spain were notable examples of the termination of democratic political processes and their replacement by national socialist dictatorships, commonly labelled Fascist. Britain, France, the United States, the Scandinavian countries, the British dominions overseas and the liberal democracies of Latin America such as Argentina all experienced a great change in the concerns of government. The problems of mass unemployment, large-scale financial and industrial failure, declining productivity and the collapse of world markets obliged all democratic governments to seek solutions for the disaster. Naturally, there was much bafflement about the problems, many ineffective nostrums suggested and much blind experimentation undertaken in response to the plea from the sufferers: 'For God's sake do something!' Hindsight tells us that many mistakes were made, and many wrong answers given to the right questions and many wrong questions asked to which no answers were possible. The total effect of all this was to bring governments more actively into economic and social affairs, and broaden very greatly ideas about what are and are not the proper concerns for government. Out the window went notions of minimal government, concerned only with law and order, diplomacy and defence, the protection of property and contracts, the preservation of sound money and the performance of all the tasks of government at the least possible cost and with the least possible borrowing on public account. The notion of positive government emerged, committed to managing the economy, planning its development and providing for all citizens from the cradle to the grave in sickness and in health, in employment and out of it.

Representative and responsible government, whenever it flourished, had always an element of jobbery in it. Those who supported the politicians in office as a result of elections were often rewarded by the government; in the United States with land grants, tariff-protection and 'jobs for the boys' as customs officers, postmen and judges; in Britain with honours, knighthoods and ennoblement or promotion up the ladder of the aristocracy, the Church and the law. Jobbery of this description affected only the comparatively small number of people who were interested and active in political life. The vast majority lived their own lives, working, trading, inventing and looking after themselves as best they could. When businessmen failed, they went bankrupt. When workers lost their jobs, they were unemployed until they found other jobs. All were expected, and most did, to provide for ill health and old age by private insurance schemes and pension funds. Those who did not do so were dependent on charity. Before the 1930s the only large-scale public services provided by the state in the United States were education and municipal services such as sanitation, public roads, street lighting and the protection of life and property. In Europe the extent of the public provision of welfare was greater than in the United States and had long been so in Germany and from 1906 in Britain, but such welfare programmes as there were assumed that most people looked after themselves and expected and wanted to do so.

As a result of the depression and then of the massive rearmament necessary to meet the challenge of Germany, Italy and Japan, the role of government in the real democracies grew enormously. The taxing and borrowing power of the United States Government, for example, was used to finance great public enterprises like the Tennessee Valley Authority, which produced electric power, reclaimed land for agriculture and restored forests destroyed by careless and improvident exploitation. In Britain in the 1920s and 1930s, publicly owned enterprises like the British Broadcasting Corporation, the Central Electricity and the London Passenger Transport Boards were organised and financed by government. Publicly owned housing was instituted. Everywhere traditional public works such as highways were expanded. State systems of insurance against unemployment and ill health were instituted and subsidies were provided for families and old people.

The experience of the Depression of the 1930s suggested that public finance could be used as a means of managing whole economies, and that by a system of large public spending in 'bad times', recession could be cured and by increasing taxation and cutting public spending in 'good times' booms and subsequent recession could be avoided. This system of fiscal management is associated with the name of the great English economist, John Maynard Keynes, whose book *The General Theory of Employment, Interest and Money*, published in 1936, became the Bible for those who believed that fiscal controls exercised by governments were the answer to depression, unemployment, poverty and distress.

Judging by the expansion and prosperity experienced in the real democracies from the close of World War II in 1945 to the onset of depression in the 1970s, Keynes and his followers were right. Fiscal management did work to the advantage of society as a whole.

Fiscal policy, however, required for its successful conduct trained and competent administrators and the support and leadership of politicians capable of understanding and working a system which required the self-discipline not only to spend when circumstances required but also to increase taxes and cut back expenditure and public borrowing when prosperity was producing nearly full employment.

By the late 1960s there began to emerge in the real democracies among both the leaders and the people themselves a spirit, which the Greeks call *hubris* and the Christians pride and vanity. The tide of easy prosperity and material abundance bred thoughtlessness and immorality, so that all began to forget the conditions and policies which must be observed to sustain economic wellbeing and development; that claims to personal income must be matched by production; that public revenue and public borrowing cannot be infinitely expanded and that even clear air and pure water have a price.

Contributing powerfully to the thoughtlessness bred of prosperity was the political processes of the real democracies. To get elected, politicians must recruit support. It became evident that the most effective way to win support in a democracy is to make promises to more and more people. Promises have a cost if they are to be implemented. Every class and every interest were led to expect they could share in the bounty of government. Spending public money became a panacea for every ill and the answer to every hope. The best reasons could always be found for the worst public extravagance. The general excuse for the soaring claims on government was compassionate regard for the poor and the disabled. In fact, however, the poor, the disabled and the unemployed were not the principal beneficiaries of government spending. The biggest pressure groups with the most influence on decision-making got the most benefits.

The competition between politicians and parties for office and power resulted in auction politics. Who will benefit whom most? The controls necessary for the operation of a system of fiscal management were abandoned. In 1973 the United States, the strongest economic power, destabilised the US dollar as an international exchange currency tied to gold. Gentle inflation, which was a feature of fiscal management, became soaring inflation. Real wages of the most vulnerable and least-organised sections of the wage-working and middle classes began to decline. Unemployment began to effect every class of society. The inflated myths about the power of government to do anything and everything were punctured.

The worship of government and an extravagant faith in its capacity to do what the authors of constitutional democracy never expected is no part of the ideology of real democracy. Liberalism (with a small 'l' and not to be confused with the term 'liberalism' as it is misused in the United States and as it applied to political parties in Britain, Canada and Australia) is the nearest the real democracies have to an ideology, but the central ideas of a liberal view of politics eschews orthodoxies of any kind, and always implies scepticism about the activities of even the best governments. In a liberal society there can be no uniformity of ideas about society, politics or policies. The core of liberalism involves an acceptance of procedures for electing representatives, determining who constitutes the executive power and the rules governing their

behaviour. What emerges from these procedures as policy is determined by the bargaining among representatives, the influence of the
executive leaders and the ability of the political activists to get sufficient support to make their policies workable as rules governing
society. In real democracies, terror and indoctrination are excluded as
means of control from the top down, just as they are excluded by law as
means to coerce government and influence elections. Real democracy
means government with the consent of the governed, freely given and
freely withdrawn.

The problems of the real world are always politico-economic in
character and men's judgement and actions are shaped by their
historical and ideological approach to this reality. Thus, central to the
study of politics and its practice is ideology, defined in its simplest
terms ·as the ideas and values that men hold—their origins, their
intellectual justification and their application.

Note: A vivid and informative example of how an individual can move
from one ideological position to another is to be found in the successive
books of the distinguished American scholar and author, James
Burnham. In the 1930s he was editing *The New International* (the
chief theoretical journal of the so-called Trotskyists). In 1983 he was
awarded the Medal of Freedom by President Reagan!

7 Politics is about the Use and Abuse of Information

Many years ago in the early days of the public relations industry, there lived in California an advertising man who thought it might be profitable and fun to specialise in promoting candidates for public office. For an agreed fee, this advertising man undertook to have clients elected to the state legislature or to any public office of the clients' choice. All he required of clients, apart from his fees, was an undertaking not to interfere in the election and to follow his instructions obediently and completely.

The advertising man's first success was an aspiring politician named Campbell. He instructed Mr Campbell to say nothing and do nothing during the election, because Mr Campbell had an unsuspected advantage upon which the advertising man proposed to build an electoral success, i.e. his name was the same as that of a famous and widely advertised brand of canned soup. In order to exploit this advantage the advertising man prepared advertisements on billboards, in the newspapers and on the television screens which urged the people to vote for Campbell. The date of the election was stated clearly and the places of voting indicated. The trick in advertising was to give great prominence to the word 'Campbell' and to display it in a script very like that of the Campbell soup brand-name, and to use a colour combination characteristic of the soup advertisements.

The advertising man was careful that this client did not confuse the voters or alienate any of them with statements about public issues, or by identifying himself with any political party. He wanted to associate the virtues of his client with the virtues of the soup. He succeeded. Mr Campbell was elected.

This may seem an extreme example of political absurdity. It is, but it also helps to identify a problem in politics everywhere: the problem of the use and abuse of information. Like most factors in human life and wellbeing such as physical strength, intelligence, natural resources, inherited social position and the random factor—luck—information about and interest in politics is unevenly distributed. Some know more

139

and care more about politics than others, and this yields advantages in the matter of gaining power and enjoying the advantages therefrom. This is particularly so in the modern world, where information about everything is more abundant and more quickly available than at any time in history.

A ruling minority—and, inevitably, rulers are a minority—with an absolute control of information occupies a very privileged position. Like the possession of armed forces, the control of information is clearly an advantage to those in whose hands it rests. With armed forces, governments can eliminate or contain internal opposition and foreign threats, but by the use of information governments can create obedience to authority, condition the public conscience and implant in the minds of people both at home and abroad a positive support for government or at least neutrality in respect to its activities. In both the democracies and the pseudo-democracies information is a critical factor in politics at least as, and perhaps more, important than the armed forces and/or the police. Indeed, the distinction between a real democracy and a pseudo-democracy turns upon the availability of information and how it is used.

The problem of information in the political life of society is more complicated and difficult than, at first sight, seems the case. To begin with, its uneven distribution is inevitable and natural, and not necessarily and always the result of conscious and deliberate action on the part of governments, private interests or organisations such as churches. Nobody can know everything and many do not want to know anything. Furthermore, therefore there is a disposition, strong in some and weak in others, to make up their own information. Obviously, the voters in California who were persuaded to vote for Mr Campbell on the assumption that he was as good and reliable as the soup whose brandname resembled his own were not well informed and/or very interested in what they were doing in voting for him. In behaving as they did, they were in no way unique, nor was their political behaviour extraordinary. Voters have frequently voted for candidates on the strength of the candidate's association with things, or institutions or beliefs of which they approve but which have little or no bearing upon what the candidate, if elected, may or may not do when active as a legislator or an executive or a judge. People have been known to vote for candidates for no better reason than that they are Catholics, or Protestants or women or white men. Indeed, an electoral phenomenon of the present day is the single-issue candidate, i.e. the candidate iden-tified with groups whose minds are obsessed by a single value or issue to the exclusion of all the decisions which may confront elected poli-ticians. Mr Campbell's electoral victory is only unique in that his public relations adviser identified him with soup. It is worth remarking, however, that the triumph of single-issue candidates is frequently a one-off event, and electors are not for very long completely gullible. As President Lincoln once remarked: 'You can fool some of the people all the time, and all the people some of the time, but you cannot fool all of the people all the time.'

Real democracy is based upon the belief rooted in experience that the people are not totally ignorant fools. It does not follow, however, that the voters are all well informed, are all capable of understanding and analysing the information available to them or even want to know and to think about political questions. Curiously enough, pseudo-democracy is based upon a belief in the intelligence of the people. That is why in the pseudo-democracies, strenuous efforts are made to control information, restrict its range and continuously interpret its meaning. The governments of the pseudo-democracies, in fact, pay the people a more handsome compliment than the politicians of the real democracies because they assume that if information is not closely controlled the people are too intelligent to support them, and the use they will make of an unrestricted flow of information will be dangerous to the authority and power of those in office. In this, governments of the pseudo-democracies are right.

Unfettered access to information and its unrestricted distribution has long been a central concern of those fostering the development of real democracy. The radical critics of the Constitution of the United States agreed to support its acceptance provided amendments were made, among the most important purpose of which was a constitutional guarantee that government does not interfere with the freedom of speech or of the press; and that the information contained in the private papers of individuals is not made available to government except in accordance with legally issued warrants of authority.

Until the Americans established their Constitution there were no general rules anywhere which guaranteed some degree of freedom of information. It was an accepted belief that those in authority had the power, which in practice was variously used, to control information by censorship, the prohibition of the publication of books deemed dangerous to the government or religion or morals, and the licensing of books and news-sheets. Hobbes' notion that one of the duties of the sovereign was to define the truth and oblige the subjects of government to accept it was not considered eccentric or strange doctrine.

It was, however, challenged by Hobbes' contemporary, John Milton. When Parliament attempted after its first victories in the Civil War to license the printing of books, Milton spoke out. His *Areopagitica* was the first, as it is the noblest, statement of the case for freedom of information and of its importance in the development of knowledge and in the cultivation of character and understanding in individuals. 'Give me,' he said, 'the liberty to know, to utter and to argue freely, according to conscience, above all liberties.' Milton said something else about information. Attempts to control it by licensing is like the exploits of that gallant man who thought to 'pound up the crows by shutting the park gate'. Censorship and licensing of information does not work very well.

So strong and so well established was the notion that those in authority ought to control information that Parliament naturally assumed that its proceedings, like all activities of government, ought to be kept a secret and known only to its own members. But Milton was right. The Members of Parliament could not 'pound up the crows', no matter how high they built the park gates. What was said in Parliament was reported and often misreported in pamphlets, news-sheets and what came to be known as newspapers. In the end Parliament had to admit that the public not only ought to know but would inevitably find out what was said in the Palace of Westminster. In 1778 a motion to proceed against violators of the orders of the House of Commons was lost. In the end Parliament authorised the printing and publication of verbatim records of its debates, now known as *Hansard*, after Luke Hansard, who first printed them.

Parliament's resolution finally to publish true, verbatim information was an attempt to solve a problem which is central to the public circulation of information, one which is still very much with us, still not solved and is probably insoluble, i.e. what is true information?

In the case of Parliament and its proceedings, the problem was comparatively easy to solve. Shorthand reporters, of whom Charles Dickens was one, took down what was said in Parliament, and these reports were published. What was said was not necessarily true, but the report of what was said was authentic and not the product of the imagination or spite or political calculation of reporters and editors. Much less simple is the problem of ensuring accuracy and truth in information generally. Adolf Hitler was expert in, but not the inventor of, the Total Lie. The technique of the Total Lie is to invent a statement which study suggests people might like to hear, but which commonsense, experience and existing information teaches is absolute and total nonsense. Once the Total Lie is invented, it is spread by every means possible. But bit by bit the Total Lie will become half-believed, then very much believed and finally the Truth, because very few people have the courage or the energy to contradict what the majority believe or want to believe. The Total Lie about the conspiracy of the Jews to

The impressive effect of the Total Lie. Hitler speaking at a massive Nuremberg rally in the late 1930s

control the world is an example of Hitler's handiwork as an inventor of Total Lies and as a propagandist.

That Hitler was able to establish a Total Lie as public truth depended upon his control of the media, the newspapers, radio stations and the means of holding meetings and demonstrations. In the first stages of his rise to power, Hitler and his propaganda expert, Joseph Goebbels, possessed only some newspapers, and access to some radio stations and public meeting-places. So long as this was so, the success of his Total Lie depended upon its capacity to evoke belief among some of the German people. Once he reached the point where he could suppress all means of critical comment on and answers to his nonsense, he could then make the Total Lie into the Truth to such a degree that even the best-informed German could not do more than remain silent in the presence of the Total Lie and the bestial consequences of his beliefs in social action and foreign policy. It is a small consolation to say that a Total Lie destroyed millions of Germans, their state and their reputation, once very high, as the most learned and cultivated in Europe.

Truth in information is perhaps the most important factor in human life; at least as important as public sanitation and personal hygiene. But how to achieve it and preserve it and make it available to everyone? Milton gave us a clue to a correct answer.

There has always been a strong tendency to believe that truth is established by authority, by a Ministry of Truth or by a learned society, or by some officer or official body capable of guaranteeing the accuracy and authenticity of what is said, or written or broadcast. The assumption that there is somewhere an official or genuine truth underlies the philosophies of all monopolies of information, be they Churches, or broadcasting organisations or private or public monopolies in the information and educational fields.

Organisations controlling newspapers, broadcasting networks, computer banks and educational systems may tell the truth either as a matter of policy or by accident, but truth is never, and never has been, a settled body of facts, ideas and information which somebody or some group can guard and disseminate. Truth is an aspiration which is never fully achieved, nor is it static and unchanging. Truth emerges, as Milton suggested, from its free pursuit, from 'promiscuous reading' and, as we might say, from being able to view independent television channels, each offering their versions of truth about which the public may decide. Equally, it requires a diversity of educational institutions, a severalty of universities and research organisations and, above all, freedom of expression, publication, broadcasting and meeting. The achievement of truth in information is a competitive process, because no-one possesses, or can possess, the whole truth.

Real democracy involves a process of determining what is true and desirable by counting opinions about facts and/or alternatives freely presented to the whole body of citizens. To suppose, however, that truth about facts can be determined in this way is, beyond a certain point, a vicious doctrine. A majority opinion cannot make white black; it can, in an instance like this, do nothing more than change the words which describe the capacity of a substance either to reflect no light or to reflect all of it. The fact will remain that there are substances which differ radically in their capacities, and if the words 'black and white' are used metaphorically when applied to actions or character, the same is true. The words can be changed by popular opinion or by governments but not the distinctions or phenomena which words describe.

When the question of what is desirable is posed to the people in a real democracy, the problem is more complex than it is when facts alone are involved. When Prime Minister Chamberlain returned from Munich after his conference with Adolf Hitler in September 1938 he declared he had achieved 'peace in our time'. His agreement with Hitler was enormously popular in Britain. The majority overwhelmingly supported him, and there is much evidence that so did the majority of the German people. Within a year Chamberlain had declared war on Germany. Obviously, majority opinion about the desirability of peace did not bring peace. The minority who were sceptical about Chamberlain's agreement with Hitler were proven right by events, and the majority wrong.

Because there is a connection between what is true in terms of facts and what is desirable or undesirable, it is important that the process of discovering factual truth and its free diffusion be not impeded or interfered with by authority or monopolies or interest groups. Unfortunately, in politics what is conceived as desirable often prevails over what facts suggest are impossible or dangerous or self-defeating. There is no easy way around this problem. Political passions often destroy the apprehension of facts. In war this is especially the case. Facts about the consequences of war are often thought to undermine morale. Therefore, facts are suppressed, not just to baffle the enemy but to prevent the people from knowing the consequences of their own actions. When by the end of 1916, intelligent men and women could see that the immense slaughter taking place could in no way justify the war in progress, the peace initiative of men like Lord Lansdowne and Ramsay Macdonald was overwhelmed by the desire for victory, and this was equally the case in Germany and in Russia. No cessation of

Chamberlain returning in triumph at London Airport, holding the Munich agreement, the final paragraph of which read: 'We are resolved that the method of consultation shall be the method adopted to deal with any other questions that may concern our two countries, and we are determined to continue our efforts to remove possible sources of difference and thus to contribute to assure the peace of Europe.' A year later, Europe was at war

hostilities was possible. Instead, the Western allies sought to play what they supposed was a high card, i.e. the involvement of the United States on their side. This produced something called victory, but it did not bring lasting peace. Within twenty years the struggle was renewed in an even more destructive form than it had had in 1914–18. In all of this, the actions of the politicians had the majority support of the people of Britain, Germany and Russia. Even the French politicians, who saw the dangers and had no stomach for a repetition of World War I, allowed themselves to be engulfed, and the majority of Frenchmen supported Daladier when he decided to fight, and Pétain when he decided to surrender seven months later.

The popular notion that majority opinion is always right, and that public opinion polls always reveal what is desirable and therefore what must be done is a serious error. What is thought desirable must be considered in relation to facts, and if this is not done, tragedy is a likely consequence.

Essential as the truthful information is in political life and indispensable as it is in the preservation and working of real democracy, there is still a serious problem even when information is freely available and is fully used in the making of decisions about public policy. Elections and public-opinion polling can only reveal what is desired. They cannot tell us what is right or wrong, i.e. what course of action will produce long-term wellbeing for individuals or for society as a whole.

This incapacity arises from the nature of information itself. Information is never complete, and even the vast abundance of information at our disposal is unknowable either to an individual or to society as a whole. In order to live and survive as a species, *homo sapiens* requires what would appear to be at first sight a contradictory and impossible kind of information: a knowledge of the unknowable. This is why there are those who believe that religion is essential in fixing the limits of human desires and thus of establishing the boundaries of choices which human beings can usefully and practically consider and to seek to realise, on the basis of their information about the material and social world. Without knowledge of the divine and the distinction between good and evil which flows therefrom, *homo sapiens* falls into incoherence, confusion and hell. Arguments of this kind demand serious consideration.

Observers of contemporary society are much puzzled by the growth of crime, violence, drug-abuse, pornography, drunkenness and insanity in which, by any rational calculation, ought to be healthy, secure and happy communities. It is possible and popular to suppose that social malaise is a by-product of war, or capitalism or disorders of the social structure; that alterations in social structure can rescue people from the hell of their own or others' making. Observation, however, does not support such suppositions.

Let us consider two communities: Sweden and Switzerland. Both are European communities, racially homogeneous and technologically advanced. Neither has known war for nearly two centuries. Sweden, unfortunately, is experiencing a growth in crime, mental disorder, drunkenness, etc. In Switzerland, on the other hand, there cannot be observed any significant change in social behaviour. The Swiss remain a peaceful, non-violent, prosperous and sober people. Why is this? Something at least can be attributed to the fact that the Swiss are still a religious people, i.e. a people among whom the Christian religion is taken seriously by a sufficient number to preserve a knowledge of the distinction between right and wrong, good and evil, coming from God, whose properties and character we can only take on trust by an act of faith.

A similar descent into hell can be observed in Britain, in the United States and in the USSR. Differences in policies, social structures and political constitutions do not explain this phenomenon common in varying degrees to otherwise dissimilar communities. Common to all of them, again in varying degrees, is the assumption upon which their decision-making is based, i.e. that the information they have about the material and social world is sufficient for the making of choices about what to do. In Britain, the United States and the USSR the knowledge of, and respect for, divine knowledge has much diminished, and in the USSR active steps over many years have been taken to eliminate a knowledge of good and evil from the community. In Britain and the United States the diminution of this knowledge and respect for it has set in for more complex reasons and not primarily from deliberate actions by the state. Rather in Britain and the United States over-confidence in the information generated by the natural and social sciences has diminished the respect for, and knowledge of, God. The knowledge of good and evil does not much influence the choices made in the framing of public policies. Legislators cannot readily recognise the face of evil because the emotional and psychological capacity has been eroded by too much faith in scientific information and too little in God.

Paradoxically, the problem of divine knowledge and information about good and evil is less in the USSR than it is in the real democracies. In the USSR the state is militantly godless and periodically seeks to destroy religious faith, or to use the Orthodox Church to sidetrack religious enthusiasm and make it an instrument of politics. As a result, the abundant failures of the state to make full use of scientific and technological information for the benefit of the community at large is associated in the popular mind with enmity to God, so that belief in God and scepticism about the state are united. This provides the grounds for Solzhenitsyn's belief that the Soviet people may in the end be the saviours of the human race. To a certain extent, events in Poland offer some confirmation of the emancipatory effect of religion in the sphere of politics.

In the real democracies the knowledge of good and evil is as much available as other kinds of information. The problem is how to bring it to bear on the making of choices. This requires a struggle to preserve freedom of information, and particularly freedom of education and freedom of religion.

Now let us consider freedom of education and freedom of religion.

Education is, or should be, concerned principally with imparting and developing skill in communication and analysis: the reading, writing and vocabulary of one's own language and of the language of other peoples; in the use of mathematical procedures; in a grasp of the methods of science; and finally in a knowledge of good and evil. How much skill is acquired in these endeavours depends upon the intelligence and character of those being educated as well as upon the capacity of teachers to teach. One thing is certain. Little can be achieved if it is not recognised by all concerned—both the teachers and the taught—that education is both an important and difficult business for all, and that if too much attention is paid to non-essentials or to political indoctrination or the acquisition of peripheral skills, the student is deprived of the fullest capacity he or she possesses to live in a complex society and to make themselves into people capable of living the lives they consider desirable.

How one approaches the problem of education depends to a considerable measure upon one's political outlook and values. In a real democracy the judgement of the people, whether as voters, or consumers or workers or entrepreneurs and business people, is the beginning of government, not its result. The acquisition of skill in acquiring information and understanding it is, therefore, of critical importance in the democratic political process. 'Education,' said Lord Brougham, a Lord Chancellor early in the nineteenth century, 'makes a people easy to lead, but difficult to drive; easy to govern but impossible to enslave.'

What is a well-conceived educational undertaking? A book on politics is not the best place for the description of a good school. In any event, descriptions of a good school are bound to differ. This is a key fact, and the one of which full account must be taken. A diversity of schools is as important in a real democracy as a diversity of newspapers, a diversity of artists, a diversity of broadcasting establishments. Good education is not a fixed procedure, the knowledge of which belongs to some individuals or some groups and not to others. It is an aspiration. Like truth, it emerges from seeking it through a diversity of approaches and a variety of insights. It is much easier to identify bad education than to define good. Once one begins to talk of an educational system one is supposing the existence of a systematiser, and a systematiser is bound to have a purpose in mind like President Kalinin, whom we have quoted. 'Literature and art,' Mao Tse-tung argued, 'fit well into the whole revolutionary machine as a component part . . . they operate as powerful weapons for uniting and educating the people and for attacking and destroying the enemy . . .'

We have to ask ourselves whether such is the purpose of art, literature and education? The answer is plainly no. Art, literature and, beyond a certain point, education are about the unknown, and only become significant after the artist, writer and teacher have shown to their fellow-men and women what they have done. Unlike the artist or writer, however, we can ask of a teacher what has been done to impart to students the skills they need to live in our society, but the imponderable influence of teachers can only be judged after they have performed their tasks. For this reason, it is contrary to the preservation of real democracy to place in the hands of political leaders the power to define education and to systematise it; to decide who teaches and what is taught.

The place of religion in society presents difficulties. We have lamented the decline in the knowledge of good and evil in our society and the tendency to assume that men and women have all the information necessary for the solution of the problems of living. Unfortunately, divine knowledge and information about the will of God is susceptible to differences of interpretation in the same way, and even to a greater extent, than less exalted forms of information. Priests are but men. Some are shepherds of the flock, but some become butchers. Some, too, regard the office of shepherd as more important than the duties. And they can differ sharply and even murderously with one another in their interpretation of divine knowledge: Roman Catholics versus Orthodox Catholics; Catholics versus Protestants; Christians versus Jews; Sunnis versus Shiites; and so on and so on. Religious enthusiasms can develop into barbarous fanaticism. Divine knowledge is necessary to men and women, but in their hands it is as lethal as atomic knowledge.

How to use it? The best general answer is: prevent monopoly and keep religion separate from politics. Religion as a still, small voice counselling men and women about their limitations, about the consequences of their self-love and their arrogance is as necessary as medical science for human life; as an encouragement to seek power in this world religion it is a plague. The crimes committed in the name of God are as innumerable as those committed by the atheists.

This is why the separation of religion from politics in the First Amendment of the Constitution of the United States is one of the most important innovations in the history of political institutions. On the least reckoning, the rule that 'Congress shall make no law respecting the establishment of religion, or prohibiting the free exercise thereof . . .' is important because it eliminates from political life contention about religion. Religion belongs to the people, and is no part of the business of government. The knowledge of good and evil and information about the pursuit of goodness and the avoidance of wickedness is a divine gift which people can seek but which cannot be forced upon them by other men and women. Freedom and non-interference by governments is as indispensable to those seeking divine knowledge as it is to scientists, artists, teachers, journalists or participants in political life. The idea of an official religion is as much a nonsense in a real democracy as the idea of a state-owned and controlled publishing monopoly or broadcasting monopoly or education system.

Experience strongly suggests that true, reliable information is necessary for life. No-one can make up his or her own information and safely and prudently rely upon such information for doing anything. Information is only reliable and said to be true when it has been passed through a scrutinising and validating process, which may be rigorously formal, as it is in a scientific laboratory, or, as is more often the case, subjected to a variety of criticisms by a variety of people. Just as scientific enquiries do not always work or may be ill conducted, scrutiny and critisism do not always produce reliable and true information. But the process of study, the accumulation of observations, analysis and then criticism is the only procedure we have which, on balance, yields good results measured in terms of successful application. Far from seeking the uniformity of doctrine to be defined by the sovereign as prescribed by Hobbes and practised by Lenin and Stalin, truth in information depends upon the multiplication of differences. We need information, but we do not need one orthodox Church. We need scientific information but we do not need an orthodox science establishment. We need schools but we do not need an educational system. We need book publishers, but not a state publishing corporation or a private monopoly in the book trade. And so on. The role and duty of government in a real democracy is to ensure the rights of every source of information, imagination or analysis to be heard. To the extent that any person or group is silenced by official or by private means by so much is the discovery of truth diminished. Of course, people have false information, mad imaginings and faulty methods of analysis. Falsity, madness and error are discovered and corrected by free discussion, not by the appointment of government inspectors, the banning of ideas and the restriction of discussion.

8 Politics is about Humanity's Unstable World

An important clue to the origins of politics is to be found in two very different works, one by a well-known scientist of the twentieth century and the other by the nameless author of Genesis, the first book of the Bible. In *The Ascent of Man* Professor J. Bronowski writes: 'Among the multitude of animals which scamper, fly, burrow and swim around us, man is the only one who is not locked in his environment. His imagination, his reason, his emotional subtlety and toughness, make it possible for him not to accept the environment but to change it.' In metaphysical language, the story of the Garden of Eden makes the same point. Eve bit into the apple on the tree of knowledge. She, her mate Adam and their descendants have had problems ever since. That is what politics is about: the problem of choice which arises because we have the power to create. To create what?

Homo sapiens can do to the environment and one another what other animals cannot. The creative power of human beings is evident everywhere around us: in art, in technology, in social and political organisations and in the remains from the past. And the problems which arise from this creative capacity are everywhere present, too.

When men and women have meditated upon their character and the likely outcome of what they do they have tended to come to two incompatible general conclusions: one pessimistic in its psychological consequences and the other optimistic. Unfortunately, there is much evidence for both conclusions.

The great religious leaders have tended towards pessimism. Men and women depending on their own powers and seeking to satisfy their desires get into grave and serious difficulties. The way out is to acknowledge a divine, unseen power, to do Its will and to follow Its way. The evidence suggests that the religious response does not limit man's creativity. In fact, it inspires it, but along certain lines. Temples and cathedrals are evidence of creativity shaped and guided by religion. Power-stations and moon-rockets are likewise evidence of creativity but shaped and guided by what?

153

Evidence for a pessimistic conclusion on the outcome of what man can do?
Unburied Nazi concentration camp victims at Buchenwald in 1945

'Well,' it is argued, 'advanced technology based on scientific enquiry is evidence that *homo sapiens* knows the score; that human beings are in control and a heaven of our own making cannot be far off. The golden age is not in the past. It is in the future. The notion of human perfectibility advanced by thinkers in the seventeenth and eighteenth centuries in Europe has something to be said for it. Paradise on earth is in prospect and this is all our own doing.'

Or maybe our undoing. In spite of the abundance of our technology, there is no evidence that human perfectibility is inevitable or even possible. The word 'perfectibility' applied to *homo sapiens* is probably a nonsense. An aspiration to perfection is reasonable enough, but if it is an aspiration, this supposes human effort towards a goal, and this excludes inevitability. Furthermore, experience shows that the conception of perfection is not one about which there can be agreement or ever has been. Plato's conception of perfection, advanced over 2000 years ago, is as much open to question as Marx's, which goes back little more than a century. Indeed, both notions of perfection are those of a beehive; all right for bees but not for human beings and nothing more than a hankering after a return to an animal condition in which no-one has a responsibility for anything, in which we all know our places and have fixity in a social order we never made. Some are willing to cherish such a conception of perfection, but many do not. It follows that such a conception is not of universal applicability and can only be established by force applied by those who believe in it at the expense of those who do not.

If we conceive of human life as an endless adventure we can take pride in our achievements and enjoy the journey in spite of ignorance or dispute about a destination. Our main concern is to keep moving, to avoid disaster and to enjoy the experience of living. This is both difficult and satisfying.

The difficulties of the adventure spring from the road we are obliged to travel. In this book we have described these as our natural necessities. About these we have no choice. We have to eat. We have to reproduce ourselves, care for our young and help them to become independently able to travel on their own. We have to work in order to extract from our environment what is necessary for our lives. Finally, we have to co-operate with one another in order to work, and to participate in the adventure.

From this it would seem that we have no choice and must bow to necessity. But to do so is not human. The capacity and inclination to make choices are among the characteristics which spring from our endowment of reason and imagination. Because these capacities and inclinations are not uniform and do not manifest themselves as similar and parallel to one another, they produce contradictions and differences, which are the origins of politics.

Over their long history men and women have developed a vast variety of methods for imposing some order upon the chaos, actual or potential, which can and often does arise from the determination of individuals and groups freely to choose what they do and how they do it.

In our world there are two approaches to the problem of order. One is the collectivist approach of the socialists, Communists and military dictatorships. The other is that of free enterprise, which is central to the working of the real democracies. Students of politics must acquaint themselves with these two approaches and understand them in order themselves to make an intelligent choice about their lives.

Both approaches have this in common. They are addressed to the problem of order in society and in the world as a whole, for they both involve a recognition of the fact evident in history that, without order, life becomes dull, brutish and short.

A key word in the collectivist approach is planning. In any human enterprise, from making a garden to drilling for oil in the ocean, it is necessary to draw upon the information connected with the undertaking and to make this information operational: to assemble the tools and resources, to introduce an effective order in their use and to distribute the end-product of the activity. This process involves planning. Without planning, nothing can be done, even if the activity has no purpose except the satisfaction of the activity itself, for example, writing a poem or playing a game. Planning is, therefore, an acceptable word simply because planning occurs in everything we do, and in a high percentage of instances, planning yields desirable results.

If one can plan a garden or an oil-drilling enterprise why not plan everything? Why not plan a society? Why not plan the world? This is the collectivist approach.

Planning requires a planner. Who is this going to be? What is the purpose of the plan? So long as the planning is specific to a particular activity it only means making decisions from a limited range of choices and concerns only the limited number of people engaged in the enterprise. When, however, planning is attempted on a large scale and embraces a whole society the choices open to the citizens are reduced. Society begins to resemble a beehive. Each has a place and an activity prescribed by the plan, and that is that. Beyond a certain point, planning is as open to the same objection as any monopoly. Planning and monopoly reduce or eliminate choice. The problems arising from freedom of choice are solved by eliminating choice. There may be some advantages in this, but we have to ask ourselves what they are.

Planning a whole society involves the assumption that someone or some group of people know what to do and how to do it. Is there any evidence for this assumption? When an individual plans a garden, he or she assumes they know what is involved in gardening. They may be wrong. The garden may yield nothing and turn out to be an eyesore. So what? Such a failure affects very few people. Even when the enterprise is a large one, such as drilling for oil in the ocean, it is possible that those who plan the enterprise will make mistakes; will not find oil; will build platforms that upset in gales; will produce more oil than the world needs; etc., etc. The loss may be considerable, but it is not a disaster for society.

When, however, a *society* is planned, everyone is involved. Disasters ramify through the whole society, and benefits are concentrated where the power is, i.e. in the hands of the planners. The Soviet Government has been planning agriculture, for example, for sixty years, and yet the Soviet Union has experienced famine on several occasions, and as recently as 1973 they have had to draw on the food stocks of the rest of the world to carry on. As it is, the unplanned part of the agricultural sector, the small plots left to the peasants for private cultivation, supplies 25 per cent of the food of the community, even though the area cultivated privately is less than 5 per cent of the cultivated land of the USSR. In this instance the small-scale planning of individual peasants seems to work, and the large-scale planning by the state seems not to do so.

Since the end of World War II a number of communities have come under the control of Marxist parties, and have become, therefore, planned societies. China, for example, has embarked on the building of a socialist/Communist society. But not all Chinese have been brought under Communist control. Taiwan, Singapore and Hong Kong are now Chinese communities where free enterprise prevails, i.e. where individuals and corporations plan their activities but the governments do not plan the economy as a whole. The contrast between the Chinese communities under Communist control and those which are not is instructive. Communist China has remained a very poor society, with a low per capita productive capacity. The non-Communist Chinese communities now have per capita gross national products from five to ten times that of the Communist Chinese.

A further example of this contrast is provided by North and South Korea. At the end of World War II the Japanese were obliged to withdraw from Korea and the Korean peninsula was divided along the 38th parallel of latitude into Soviet- and American-occupied territories. These occupation zones have now become separate independent states: the North, Communist and planned, and the South, free-enterprise and unplanned. North Korea has fewer people (less than half) than South Korea and better natural resources. None the less the productivity per head of population in South Korea is more than double that of North Korea, and this in spite of a devastating war caused by the attempt of the North Koreans to take over South Korea. Again, it would appear that planning at the individual and corporate level works and the planning of a whole society is not successful, if the measure of success is the production of goods and services.

The purpose of economic planning is supposed to be the production of goods and services on a large scale and their fair distribution in society. In the pseudo-democracies it has another purpose. It is one of the tools for the control of the people. The plan provides the only socio-economic structure in which individuals can find an opportunity to work, and the distribution of the goods and services produced are planned to recruit political support for the regime. Bread, for example, is sold at low, stable prices. This demonstrates a compassionate regard for the welfare of the mass of the people. On the other hand, the distribution of consumer durables in short supply on account of planning decisions and planning failure is determined by the issue of permits to purchase given to those in authority, to those whose technical expertise is needed by the regime and to those who might otherwise complain or criticise the way things are done or not done. In these circumstances, cheap bread is very expensive, and a motor car can cost one independence of mind even when one has the money to buy one.

When people undertake to plan a whole society, or, in the socialist manner, to establish state monopolies over the 'commanding heights' of an economy, planning inevitably becomes a tool in the political process of getting and keeping power. Let us examine in this connection the political use of sports and games.

Games and sports should have no place in a Communist or socialist society. In the first place, sports and games are competitive, and to Communists and socialists competition is a dirty word. In the second place, sports and games are based upon the proposition that all men and women are not equal. In the third place, sports and games are non-political, i.e. the outcome of sports and games cannot be determined by authority and state power.

The object of sports and games is to discover who in a community has the greatest physical skill, natural or acquired, discovered by organised contests carried out in accordance with rules. Of all forms of human activity of a non-economic kind, sports and games command the greatest interest of peoples everywhere, whether as participants or as spectators. No amount of ideological, moral or political argument can extinguish this popular addiction to sports and games, nor has anyone offered any convincing explanation of why this is so.

The government of the USSR, for example, accepts this fact. Sports and games are activities which have no political implications in themselves. There can be no Marxist way of playing ice hockey or running the hundred metres. It is, therefore, a safe, non-political human activity, which cannot bring into question great ideological truths. On the other hand, success in sports and games can be attributed to the community where success is achieved. What a perfect way of advocating the merits of Communism if Soviet sportsmen and women display talents which are universally admired and respected!

In the USSR there need be no conflict between amateur and professional, because no-one has the means to be an amateur or the need to be a professional. The state provides for all. Allocate the resources and reward the participants. All else will follow: success, esteem and self-confidence, useful politically at home and abroad. And a triumph of planning. For many years, athletes and sportsmen of the Soviet Union and the Soviet satellites have commanded the admiration of the world.

But what does all this prove? First, that planning when applied in a limited, well-defined sphere, as it is applied in free enterprise societies to all endeavours, works. Second, that excellence is discovered by competition, otherwise denied as an essential ingredient of life by the official ideology and in the practice of daily life in the Soviet Union.

Other communities have responded to the Soviet challenge in sports and games. Now it is being demonstrated that Soviet sportsmen and women win some and lose some. Marxism has nothing to do with the matter, which many people have long suspected. Nor has the total planning of society. But try telling this to a Soviet propagandist. Planners use planning as political aids in the struggle to get and keep power.

This is evident when one examines the *modus operandi* of Marxist planners in the matter of music, literature, painting and the arts generally. Like sports and games, the arts are non-economic and non-political in any direct sense. Artists, like sportsmen and women, have to eat and need equipment; to this extent there is an economic dimension to their activities, but the activities of artists of all kinds are not directed to the production of goods and services which can be fitted into anybody's plan, nor can a planner say what artists can or cannot produce.

Unfortunately, this is not the view of people planning whole societies. One can reasonably suppose that music, for example, is non-economic and non-political. It is as difficult to imagine a Marxist fugue as it is an ice-hockey game played in accordance with the principles of Michael Harrington. But Stalin could. At his direction an opera by Shostakovich was suppressed. Of course, in opera there exists the possibility of an aria with subversive implications, but not surely such notes in a concerto. None the less some of Shostakovich's instrumental orchestral works were censored, and Prokofiev had to watch his step. Just what was wrong in the minds of the Stalinist censors is not clear, but it was made plain that composers of music were not free men nor ought they to pose as such by producing work which was not understood and appreciated by the men and women in the Politbureau.

Literature, the visual arts, the theatre and the cinema do have political overtones—not always, but in some cases. They do sometimes make people think, and this is dangerous to planners, for thinking may not always confirm and strengthen the policies and practices of the authorities. Hence the need for control, guidance and censorship. Access to the tools of a trade can be controlled. Definitions of what is acceptable art can be established. Official approval of artistic productions can be required. All of this does not prohibit artistic activity, but its cumulative effect is to ensure as far as possible that art supports authority and does not cast doubt upon it.

This practice of controlling the arts and its purpose was well stated by A. A. Zhdanov. In an essay 'On Literature, Music and Philosophy' he declared: 'We demand that our comrades, both practising writers and those in positions of literary leadership, should be guided by that without which the Soviet order cannot live, that is to say, by politics, so that our young people may be brought up not in the spirit of do-nothing and don't care, but in an optimistic revolutionary spirit.'

Lest anyone suppose that this sentiment is peculiarly Russian, we have a Chinese Communist version laid down by Mao Tse-tung, already quoted, to the effect 'that literature and art fit well into the whole revolutionary machine . . .'

We have to ask ourselves whether art is part of a revolutionary machine. Even a socialist artist like William Morris would have found it difficult to think of himself as a cog in a machine or even as a whole engine. When artists can do nothing but sing the praises of authority and must accept the guidance of politicians, the power of the artist is thereby diminished. This means that humanity is robbed of the fruits of reason, imagination, and emotional subtlety. In any event, as Milton, an artist if ever there was one, has argued, censors cannot 'pound up the crows' in the long run. And what can be said to justify the practice of putting dissident artists into insane asylums to be treated as psychotic personalities?

As readers will likely have suspected, by now, the authors of this book are not neutral about freedom for the individual, no matter how many problems this may create. They are for freedom of choice, individualism and real democracy. These preferences are aspirations, because unlimited freedom of choice is not possible given the natural necessities we have described; unrestrained individualism is not possible because social co-operation is demonstrably necessary for life; and real democracy is never completely achieved. None the less, these aspirations are a guide to the practical solution of problems posed by the adventure of living, and these, readers should consider and judge for themselves.

Like Professor Bronowski, we identify reason and imagination as two distinctly human capacities. These capacities develop through use. The fundamental objection to government by a narrowly recruited and selective élite of any kind is its tendency to restrain the capacity for reasoning and imagination in the rest of the community. This is not so true when an élite group limits its activities to the bare essentials of government such as keeping order; but narrowly recruited élites held together by intellectual dogmas and bent on planning and controlling a wide span of human activities are a menace to mankind. The cramping and deadening effects of government of this kind on the cultivation of reason and imagination is debilitating. Such control by dogmatists exercising wide powers is like that of narrow-minded authoritarian and fearful parents, who never encourage their children to grow up and mature into self-sufficient adults.

Freedom to choose and willingness to accept the risks involved in choosing wrongly or in finding one's choices obstructed or denied are important factors in the development of the capacities and character of individuals and of the societies where freedom and risk-taking flourish. Choice requires imagination, even in a supermarket full of pre-packaged food, and the acceptance of risks requires courage. Imagination, reason and courage are qualities in men and women from which creativity flows and upon which abundance, understanding and survival depend. The maximising of freedom of choice and of opportunities to take risks are, or should be, the object of political action, but are often not the objects of government. Whether freedom of choice and the taking of risks are compatible with government is a central question, which readers of this book are invited to consider.

Because this is a book about politics, attention has been paid primarily to political ideas and political practices. Life, however, is not all politics. Indeed, the lives of the vast majority, though dependent upon the political structures and practices of society, are concerned with the work, play and the experience which constitute living. Freedom of choice is important in political life; in the practical life of the vast majority it is even more important.

This book cannot be complete without an examination of the way in which freedom of choice in practical living is achieved or diminished.

The experience of history strongly suggests that there is a close connection between political freedom and freedom of enterprise in the important activity of providing for our natural necessities.

In order to achieve some simplicity, clarity and moral understanding in the discussion of free enterprise, it is necessary to understand three concepts: the concept of property, of self-interest and of competition. In the vocabulary of the socialists, the Communists and the bureaucratic élite, property, self-interest and competition are dirty words, and it is a fact, sad but true, that the vocabulary of the Left is now the dominant vocabulary in parts of the Western world: in the schools and institutions of higher education, in the media, in politics and in the churches. Property, self-interest and competition have become taboo subjects, much as the public discussion of anything to do with sex was taboo in Victorian society,.

The concept of property supposes the right to ownership, i.e. the right of absolute control: to consume, to enjoy, to use, not to use, to lend and to exchange for property belonging to others. But ownership of what? The most fundamental piece of property a man or woman can have is his or her own person, with that person's capacity to work, i.e. to create material goods or perform services for himself or herself or for others. Work is the origin of all property, and is the most fundamental of all human activities. One who does not own his or her own person is neither free or even fully human. This is why it has been necessary to abolish slavery, which is the total ownership of persons by other persons, and feudal social relations, which involves the partial ownership of persons by other persons, in order to create a free-enterprise, market economy.

If one's own person is one's own property, this means that one has the right of disposal of the goods or services which one produces or renders. This right of disposal implies a right to use or to exchange in accordance with one's self-interest. One can, for example, exchange one's labour (i.e. the activity of providing a good or a service) for goods or services which one consumes immediately or in a short span of time, or one can exchange it (or part of it) for a promise of goods and services at some future time. Exchanging a present asset for a future asset supposes that in society there are some who do not need all their assets for their immediate needs and some who have needs in excess of their present capacity to produce goods and services. By exchanging present assets for promises to provide assets in the future, men and women are able to co-operate with one another, to develop a division of labour among themselves, and to increase the productivity of their individual labour, their co-operative activity and the use of tools of greater and greater complexity and sophistication.

Any system of exchange supposes the exchange of goods and services for goods and services. These exchanges are governed by self-interest, i.e. by the propensity to maximise one's own acquisition of goods and services. Both reason and experience demonstrate, however, that self-interest must be defined and limited. If this is not done, there exists the possibility that individuals or groups will seek to effect exchanges of nothing for something. In terms of pure self-interest this is the best exchange one can make. Such exchanges of nothing for something are most often made by force or by fraud or by both.

In order that the practice of exchanging property (i.e. the fruits of labour) for other property can be established as a means of social co-operation it is therefore necessary to develop rules or customs which exclude the use of violence and fraud, and ensure that goods and services are exchanged for goods and services.

The concept of self-interest, therefore, requires some definition. As a concept it is open-ended, but only on the assumption that the parties to an exchange have both rights *and* duties, the right to offer a good or a service and the duty to offer one which *can be refused*.

Self-interest is a deeply rooted characteristic of human beings and, indeed, of all animals, but both in its intensity and its modes of expression, self-interest is extremely variable: from the totally selfish materialist to the saint, totally divested of material and emotional desires, whose sole interest is union with God. How one defines one's self-interest and how one seeks to achieve it is in itself an aspect of self-interest.

Both reason and experience suggests that the very great variety of self-interest in individuals and collections of individuals precludes the possibility, except by chance, of a harmony or parallelism of interests. It is furthermore a matter of observation that the pursuit of self-interest can be destructive of individuals or society or both. It is, therefore, a problem for men and women generally to discover some method of containing and controlling a force so universal and so actually or potentially destructive.

Of all the solutions of this problem of self-interest, the most productive of harmony and co-operation is the set of social arrangements we call a *laissez-faire* market economy.

In the first place, a market economy involves the acknowledgement of self-interest as an important and indeed central psychic force in individuals. A market economy avoids the delusive artifice of concealing self-interest in the rhetoric of benevolence, which is the observed practice of bureaucratic empire-builders, politicians and reformers of various kinds.

In the second place, a market economy tends to focus self-interest on the necessary and predominantly healthy activity of exchanging goods and services and to divert it from political, intellectual and religious goals, which are not susceptible to agreed definition and have a capacity to generate antagonism and even destruction. Thinking and feeling about religion, philosophy, politics and art are inevitable and indispensable human activities whose character is transformed and then destroyed if they 'go public' and are made into rallying cries of contending interests. The production and exchange of goods and services, on the other hand, are both private and, through the agency of market arrangements, public activities, which, because they are both necessary and specific, have only a limited power to produce irreconcilable differences out of which spring wars and social disasters.

In the third place, a market economy breaks down and defines self-interest so that only individuals or small aggregations of individuals—associations, corporations, trade unions and so on—confront one another. Confrontation of self-interested parties in a market suppose an outcome involving some kind of shared benefits from a transaction, and whatever the shared benefits may be they are unlikely to involve the total lives and all interests of the parties to the transaction. It is quite possible in a market economy for self-interested parties confronting one another in determining the price of a commodity or the wages to be paid for a service to be otherwise friends and neighbours and fellow citizens. Even their confrontation in the market is limited and is but a stage in reaching an agreement to co-operate: to pay £x for a ton of copper or to pay £y an hour for labour or £z for a piece of technical advice. In short, a market decentralises self-interest and prevents it from aggregating and building up to the point of explosion—as collective self-interest does in political or religious confrontations.

The history of Europe and of the world during most of the nineteenth century was rather peaceful compared with its history in the eighteenth and the twentieth centuries. Perhaps the growth of market economies had something to do with this difference, and their decline in importance as central agencies of social organisation something to do with the war and rumours of wars so much present for at least three-quarters of this century.

The third concept central to any system of free enterprise is competition. This concept embraces the notion of free participation in the activity of producing goods and/or services and the exchanging of the same. A market economy is a social mechanism for making decisions about prices, i.e. the determination in terms of money of the rate at which goods and services exchange for one another. No individual or corporation can say what a price is or should be. Only the participants in a market can say what a price is or should be, although many wish they could. The participants in a market can say what a price is by stating what amount of assets one is willing to give up to acquire the goods or services on offer. The participant who makes the largest offer accepted by buyers determines the price of the good or service on offer. This price is what the seller must accept and the buyer pay. This price will determine the decisions of sellers about whether they wish or are able to produce and sell and the decisions of buyers about whether they wish or are able to continue consuming or holding or using the goods and services for sale.

The concept of competition supposes freedom in the market and freedom to enter or leave the market. Unless this freedom exists both in law and in practice, the social mechanism for the determination of prices is impaired or ceases to exist. The producers of a commodity can only discover how much to produce and what to produce if they are able to ascertain what consumers will pay them, and equally consumers can only discover what proportion of their assets they can use for buying a particular commodity or service. Furthermore, the market is a better means of achieving a match between production and consumption than any yet evolved.

All this seems obvious to anyone who has engaged in productive activity. Unfortunately, what is obvious is not widely known or understood by the large number of people in our society who are not engaged in the production of goods and services whose prices are determined by market forces. In all societies an increasing proportion of people have incomes which are not determined either directly or indirectly in the market sector. Their incomes are derived from state revenues, and these revenues are obtained in three ways: by taxation which is the transfer of assets to the government from the owners by the use of power: by borrowing in the capital market, and by inflation which is the printing of money or surrogates for money, and is a form of fraud inasmuch as it enables governments to pay with counters which represent neither goods nor services. Only in the case of borrowing does the state make the owner of assets an offer which he or she *can* refuse. Taxes are paid because governments have the power (i.e. the force) to collect them; and inflation is a fraud endured because there is no law to prevent it and no agency to enforce such a law.

Incomes derived from state revenues, like subsidies from the same source, do not arise from bargains or exchange of goods and services for goods and services. When very large numbers of people in a society rely in this way for their sustenance, even when they work at some administrative task or engage in planning or teaching, there exists in society a significantly large interest group whose members do not and cannot naturally have any knowledge of economic reality. Their self-interest expresses itself only as claims for more pay, better conditions, larger allowances and so on.

In 1978 two British economists, Robert Bacon and Walter Eltis, published an analysis of the British economy, which has never received the attention it deserves. Bacon and Eltis worked on data available in 1975. They found that the people in Britain producing goods and services numbered 19,698,000. These people supported themselves and another 5,270,000 in non-productive employment, plus 929,000 unemployed. Given the trends they observed in the British economy Bacon and Eltis predicted that by 1982 18,700,000 people would still be supporting 5,270,000 non-producers and 2,850,000 unemployed. Their prediction has come to pass, but not much attention has been paid to what they have had to say. Why?

Governments do not take advice because it is good, or scientific or true. Some governments may wish to do so, but politicians in the real democracies are obliged to do what their supporters demand, either to achieve power or to stay there. When so many supporters of government depend for their incomes or for subsidies upon government, and when the productive community is divided artificially by socialist and Communist propaganda into antagonistic groups, it is little wonder that governments can, only with difficulty, find sufficient support to restore and make work effectively a system of free enterprise based on freedom of choice. It can be done but it is difficult to do so.

Yet freedom of choice in all departments of life make it necessary to re-establish the linkage between political freedom and economic freedom. The myth that governments can do everything, pronounce on everything and always know best, must be dispelled, and the true and necessary business of governments must be redefined and the definition observed.

Why? Because man is an imperfect species in an imperfect world. That world changes whether we like it or not, and the major factor in change is the exercise and cultivation of human reason and imagination. Reason and imagination can save us or destroy us, but not the reason and imagination of a single individual or a self-selected group. Individuals and self-selected groups make mistakes as everyone does.

We cannot therefore allow a situation to develop in which the mistakes of a few bring disaster to all. On this prudent proposition rests the case for representative, responsible government and real democracy.

Select Bibliography

1. *The Current Debate—Liberal Democracy versus Marxism*
   K. Marx and F. Engels, *The Communist Manifesto*
   V. I. Lenin, *State and Revolution*
   J. V. Stalin, *1936 Constitution of the USSR*
   Mao Tse-tung, *Quotations from Chairman Mao Tse-tung*
   Den Hsiao-p'ing, *Selected Works of Den Hsiao-p'ing*
   F. A. Hayek, *The Road to Serfdom* (Routledge and Kegan Paul)
   K. W. Watkins, *The Paradise-Builders and Other Essays* (Sherwood Press)
   H. S. Ferns, *The Disease of Government* (Temple Smith)
   B. Crozier, Drew Middleton and J. Murray-Brown, *This War called Peace* (Sherwood Press)
2. *Further Reading*
   Chilperic Edwards, *Man's Earliest Laws* (Watts)
   Jack Reynolds, *The Great Paternalist* (Temple Smith)
   Adolf Hitler, *Mein Kampf*
   K. R. Minogue, *Nationalism* (Methuen)
   J. Macfarlane, *Modern Political Theory* (Nelson)
   M. Duverger, *The Study of Politics* (Nelson)
   B. Crozier and A. Seldon, *Socialism Explained* (Sherwood Press)
   Carl Henrik von Platen, *The Uneasy Truce: How Bureaucracy could Undermine Western Democracy* (Sherwood Press)
   R. N. Berki, *The History of Political Thought* (Dent)
   G. H. Sabine, *A History of Political Thought* (Harrap)
3. *The Classics*
   Plato, *The Republic*
   Aristotle, *Politics*
   Machiavelli, *The Prince* and *The Discourses*
   Milton, *Aeropagitica*
   Hobbes, *Leviathan*

Locke, *Two Treatises on Government*
Rousseau, *The Social Contract*
Burke, *Reflections on the French Revolution* and *Speeches*
Hamilton, Jay and Madison, *The Federalist* (Dent)
Mill, *On Liberty*
J. Plamenatz, *Readings from Liberal Writers* (Allen and Unwin)

Index